TO KILL A
ZOMBIE

TO KILL A ZOMBIE

THE YEAR I CAME BACK TO LIFE—*AND WHY*

DAVID W. PIERCE

LEAFWOOD
PUBLISHERS

TO KILL A ZOMBIE
The Year I Came Back to Life—And Why

Copyright 2012 by David W. Pierce

ISBN 978-0-89112-267-8
LCCN 2011046165

Printed in the United States of America

Scripture quotations, unless otherwise noted, are from The Holy Bible, New International Version. Copyright 1984, International Bible Society. Used by permission of Zondervan Publishers. Scripture quotations noted WEB are from the World English Bible, used by permission.

LIBRARY OF CONGRESS CATALOGING-IN-PUBLICATION DATA
Pierce, David W.
To kill a zombie : the year I came back to life-and why / David W. Pierce.
   p. cm.
ISBN 978-0-89112-267-8
1. Pierce, David W. 2. Christian biography. 3. Life--Religious aspects--Christianity. I. Title.
BR1725.P5143A3 2012
277.3'083092--dc23
[B]

                                                            2011046165

Interior text design by Sandy Armstrong
Cover design by Marc Whitaker

Leafwood Publishers is an imprint of
Abilene Christian University Press
1626 Campus Court
Abilene, Texas 79601

1-877-816-4455
www.leafwoodpublishers.com

12 13 14 15 16 17 / 7 6 5 4 3 2 1

As always, to my wife, Chonda.

Most men lead lives of quiet desperation.

—Henry David Thoreau, American writer

I've known of this quote for many years.
Only recently have I come to understand it.

—David W. Pierce, former zombie

Contents

. . . Even the frogs were zombies.

—from "Briar Rose," a poem by Anne Sexton
about the real Sleeping Beauty

Warning:
Zombies Are Everywhere!

Are you a zombie? Is someone you know a zombie? On the following page is a quick test you can take just to be sure.

And if you are a zombie, don't panic. I used to be one too. There is hope. *There is always hope.* But there is one thing you must be willing to do. Fortunately that thing does not involve money or a seven-step program. There is only one way to kill a zombie . . . *only one.* The remaining pages merely make a big circle around this weapon, so that you can view it from all sides.

Now, look up from this book for just a moment and make eye contact with someone there close by, a friend, a stranger—anyone. Once you've made eye contact, smile or nod or do something to let that person know that he or she, at this very moment, is not alone.

There. The zombie has already been wounded.

The Zombie Quiz

1. When you play five hours of golf with your buddies do you talk about anything besides golf?
2. Have you talked recently to a complete stranger (say, a gang member) in a dress shop?
3. Have you guffawed lately with a good friend—for an hour and half?
4. Did anyone sing happy birthday to you on your last birthday—in the jungle?
5. Have you ever shared air on the ocean floor, ninety feet underwater?
6. Have you even looked at the stars lately? With strangers?
7. Have you volunteered a body part recently—like your brain or back or heart?
8. Have you done something scary lately—say, ride a roller coaster—just because someone else wanted to?
9. Have you shared outdoor air with anyone lately?
10. Do you grab at life like a baby?

Zombie Grading Scale

There is no zombie grading scale. My guess is that if you're reading this, you failed the above quiz—miserably. No need to beat up on yourself. You need help. You need advice. You need to be encouraged that the zombie can be killed and you can be alive again. I say "again," because my guess is that you remember those days when you felt alive. You're just not sure when you died. I didn't either. I staggered through a lot of days. But I'm back. And the zombie is dead.

So read on. This is how I did it.

Prologue

The Zombie First Appears

She certainly didn't look like a monster—this woman who stood in line just ahead of me in the express lane at Walmart. The sign strapped with plastic binding to the pole at the register sounded adamant: 10 ITEMS OR LESS. (And the all-caps were theirs, not mine.)

Two lines of shoppers, all with just a handful of items, queued up waiting for the cashiers to call them to come forth. The first was fairly close to where the line ended, the other about five paces back. Customers had been trained over the years to anchor at this spot, where the woman in front of me stood, and wait until either register one or two opened up.

"Ma'am, I can take you here," a timid-looking young woman spoke from the nearest register to the woman in line in front of me. Only the *un*-monster in front of me didn't move; she never even swiveled her head. And as far as I could tell, never even shifted an eyeball in the direction of register #1. She was frozen!

I'd come in for a can of peas—to go with the roast my wife had promised to make for dinner. "Just need some peas," she'd said. And because I'd only come for peas, I hadn't grabbed one of those handy plastic baskets they have stacked at the front door. I'll carry it, I'd thought. But any time I'm called to the grocery store aisles looking for, say . . . a can of peas, I'll see something that probably should have been on the list. A loaf of bread, for instance. So I grabbed up a fresh loaf. That was easy enough to do. Keeps me balanced—cargo-wise. And I remembered we'd run out of tomato juice. (That last glass had been exquisite!) So I tucked a new bottle under the arm of the hand that carried the peas. And because I love the dogs, I remembered we were nearly out of their favorite prime steak in gravy that more than once, after opening a can, my wife would take a big, long sniff and say, "Mmmm, are you grilling something?" So I grabbed up an eight-pack and offset the weight of the tomato juice that was clamped under the other arm. All was fine, but I also needed a gallon of milk.

"Ma'am," the timid cashier tried again. "I can help you here."

I wondered if I should say something. If I just repeated "Ma'am" and gave a big hitch of my head, that would probably be enough. But just then the juice shifted and I had to re-clamp, and the gallon of milk swung from a single finger, and on the other side I grasped the dog food as if it were a giant textbook (biology, most likely, because it was so large and heavy), all the while steadying the bread in the crook of an elbow.

"Ma'am. I said I can take the next—"

"Oh my!" the woman said suddenly, as if a professional hypnotist had just counted down from ten and snapped his fingers and now she was back with us. She stepped up to register #1 and placed her basket with less-than-ten-items onto the conveyor belt. "I'm so sorry to hold you up like that. I was just standing there like a . . . like a zombie, I guess. Ha, ha ha ha ha ha ha!" The longer she laughed like that, the more zombie-like she sounded.

The timid-looking girl methodically pulled the items from the basket and scanned them, without passion.

The word "zombie" took me back. I was eighteen, a freshman in college, when one day my dad was bored and said, "Let's go see a movie." That was back before the multiplex theaters that offered up forty-seven different choices. Then, we had one screen and one choice. There was no need to call up and see what was playing. We just went.

"Sir! I can help you here."

So we drove there, bought our tickets and settled in with popcorn and drinks to watch the newly released movie: *Dawn of the Dead*, where slow-moving zombies ate people in a shopping mall. Scary stuff for the 70s. But before I could hyperventilate or toss my lunch (like I wanted to), a man somewhere near the center of the theater sprung from his seat and, in a voice that could be heard above the munching of the zombies on screen, shouted (to someone a little too close by), "Get off of me, woman!" Nervous laughs went up (mine being one of them) and for a moment the atmosphere seemed to lighten, the zombies were less threatening. That is, until they devoured an entire motorcycle gang.

"Sir! I said I can take you over here."

Oh, that was for me! I shook off the memory and took a step toward register #2, securely gripping the peas in one hand. However, the finger on the other hand, that held the milk, had gone numb, so I did a quick shift of the jug from one finger to the next, causing the weight to swing pendulum-like, causing me to have to re-grip the dog food. The bread, in its slick casing, made its escape on the inside of my arm, snaking its way down my side. So I quickly clamped it with that arm. All was still well.

Just then the dog food threatened to tear loose, so I pinched the case against my leg. The milk would not stop swinging (following some law of physics, I'm sure). My whole sense of balance suddenly threatened! The tomato juice, however, felt secure in armpit #1. I squeezed everything more tightly and leaned toward register #2, making a shuffle step that way. Step and then drag (the leg where the dog food was balanced). Step and then drag. When I made it there the timid girl asked, "Do you have your Valued Customer Card?"

In my wallet, yes. (I might have groaned.) Slowly I began to unload my goods. I unflapped one wing and let the bread drop onto the conveyor belt first. It moved away from me, wounded, unable to hide an indention the width of an average-sized male elbow in the center of its loaf. The peas I let fall to the belt with the *clunk* sound of dead weight. I pressed the dog food against the metal casing of the conveyor belt and, with hip and hands, eventually rolled the batch of cans onto the moving conveyor that pulled me along with it for a second, causing me to lean even more into the direction of the cashier. (I might have groaned a second time.) I used the pendulum motion of the milk to my advantage and landed it there behind the dog food. The tomato juice, however, I slipped from my armpit and placed it perfectly upright on the moving belt. The legless jar glided away, glistening blood red in its glass container.

Somewhere, it seemed, someone should have probably screamed.

The Zombie Is in My House!

Not long after this moment in the grocery store, I sat with my wife on our back deck that overlooks a peaceful river. I was content to wile away the minutes because I was tired and just wanted to rest for a moment. So I focused on a tree, one with a twisted branch that drooped and swung its dead leaves close to the ground. I guess the tree had me hypnotized because even though Chonda's voice was loud, only some of what she said got through. And what I did hear barely made any sense. Was she even talking about me? Then one sentence got through, stung me like ice water: "I just want you to do *something*."

I turned my gaze from the droopy branch and saw that she was on the verge of tears. I cleared my throat and said, protest-like, "I do things," but my voice sounded anemic even to me. I only protested because it seemed I was always "doing." If anything I was exhausted from the doing. That's why I was there on the deck just then: I needed the rest!

"I know, I know." She shook her head like that wasn't exactly what she'd meant. "I know you do stuff all the time. For me. For the kids. But I think it would be a good idea for you to do something . . . *for you.*"

I had no clue what she was talking about. "Like what?"

She shrugged. "I don't know. Join a club. Volunteer for something. Help people." She placed a hand on my arm and squeezed. "You've just seemed kinda . . . *dead* for a long time now."

Dead? I turned back to my swaying tree. Was she right? Had I died? And just when had that happened? A breeze moved the tree branch back and forth, so gracefully and beautifully. But the brown and yellowed leaves belied its life-like qualities. I thought about what she'd said, and I knew she was right. Sometime back I had died. I wasn't sure of the exact day, or even the year, or how long I'd been dead. All I was sure of is that my death had come slowly, little by little. I could still "do" things, like walk, button my shirt, even golf. What I hadn't been able to do for a long time was to connect with people. That's the simple answer. I couldn't feel the joy of being with others. I've always loved my children and my wife, and I'd done a pretty good job of pretending to live. But Chera had married and moved away, and Zachary was all grownup now and off to school on the other side of the country. I'd seen these changes on the horizon for some time now. And I guess the sight of them racing in had whittled away at me, until all that was left were the numb parts.

But I didn't have any real friends. I didn't talk about life (or things concerned with the living) with anyone. It was easier to grab a bite of lunch by myself, to go fishing alone, to play nine holes alone (working on my swing, I would tell myself). I was alive, but I was dead. So I really was a zombie.

I think there was a part of me that had known this to be true for some time, but I didn't think it was so noticeable. And, at first, I was afraid that Chonda had blown my cover. Or worse, that by speaking the words, she'd not only drug my zombiehood out into the open, but potentially made my condition permanent. Later, I would come to believe that she was the first to breathe life back into me.

Just then a light breeze blew across the deck, bringing with it the dry rattle of dead leaves.

So I bought a book about zombies, on a chance I could learn something about myself. I discovered that there are basically two kinds of zombies. There's the standard garden variety zombie: a corpse with basic motor skills, the kind that eat living people in shopping malls. Then there's the "philosophical zombie": a person who may look just fine, but have "no thoughts, feelings or interior life of any kind" (*The Undead* xiv).[1] And here's the scary thing about zombies. We remember that person/zombie when he was alive. We watched him at the grocery store, bumped into him at Walmart, borrowed a pressure washer from him one fall and he seemed irritated that I returned it two weeks later, played golf with him, sat two pews away from him at church recently, and saw him raise his hand at the chorus of "Shout to the Lord." *He was so alive then!* Now he's among the walking dead. Or, as some of the zombie experts refer to it, "The Undead"—not exactly dead but not exactly alive either. Trapped somewhere in between.

That's where I've been.

I didn't read any more because it was too disturbing to read about my own death. There was also a chapter in there about how to kill a zombie, but it wasn't exactly metaphorical and required a truck full of

---

1 *The Undead and Philosophy. Chicken Soup for the Soulless*, Eds. Richard Greene and K. Silem Mohammad, (Chicago, IL: Open Court Publishing, 2006).

ammunition (bullets, grenades, a cricket paddle, etc.) So I had to come up with my own plan.

The Greatest Commandment says to love God and love people. I love God. I truly believe I've had that first one down for a while now. I go to church. I have all sorts of praise music on my IPod. But it's that second part of the commandment that I've had trouble with—the people part. But people and God go together. You love God by loving people. So I figured out that by not connecting with people, I've really only loved God from a distance. Okay, I finally realized (imagine the sounds of kicking and screaming), I'm going to have to draw closer to God's people. That ought to do the trick. *That* will be the cure.

So that's what this book is about: coming back to life—*by connecting with people*. I figured I'd start "seriously connecting" first with someone I know: my son. Zachary is nineteen while I'm writing this, and he looks and acts just like me when I was nineteen. I was thirty when he was born, the same age as my father when I was born. So at every stage of his life I've played a simple game of "when I was his age. . . ." He loves rock and roll, ultimate fighting, *The Simpsons*, any superhero movie, Halo 1, 2, and 3, and giant roller coasters. He's a constant reminder to me of what it's like to be alive and engaged in life. I will reconnect with him, and that will help me to connect with others.

And since I've forgotten what it's like to be fully alive, I will go back and remember what it was like when I was connected to others. What did I have then that I don't now? Then I will leap across that gap of dryness and explore what is going on today—as a zombie. My prayer is that the gap will slowly close, and that life will begin to flow back into these dry bones.

This is the story about how one day I set out to kill a zombie, and the only ammunition I carried was a simple "hello."

~

When I heard the learn'd astronomer,

When the proofs, the figures,
were ranged in columns before me,

When I was shown the charts and diagrams,
to add, divide, and measure

them,

When I sitting heard the astronomer

where he lectured with much

applause in the lecture-room,

How soon unaccountable I became tired and sick,

Till rising and gliding out I wander'd off by myself,

In the mystical moist night-air, and from time to time,

Look'd up in perfect silence at the stars.

—Walt Whitman (1865), American poet

~

1

Close Encounter
of a Stardust Kind

Back when I was alive, my brother-in-law Mike and I took the
kids across country in a minivan. My daughter Chera was twelve and
my son was seven. Mike's boys were fourteen and ten. We left from
Ohio and were going to meet our wives in Denver, who had flown out
early because of work. So we carved out three days to camp along the
way. One night we were somewhere in Kansas and the evening air was
warm, so we decided not to pitch a tent. We pumped up our sleeping
mattresses and laid them out on some tall grass, then lined up side-by-
side like logs, and watched the night sky and counted shooting stars.
Only Zachary had a hard time spotting them. By the time I could point
and redirect his gaze, the star was gone.

"There's one!" Zach finally shouted, and he pointed. I saw it too,
bright and yellow and so close. "I see it! I see it!" His finger traced its path
across the sky. "It's coming this way! It's coming right at us!" He buried

his face in my shoulder and prepared for the crashing of the shooting star. I held him close and laughed as the lightning bug flew on past.

Yeah, I was alive then. Very much so.

As a zombie, and on campus at Middle Tennessee State University where I teach English, I watched the daily progress of a group of men as they built a small brick structure in the middle of a large grassy area. It was very small, maybe 10 X 12, and one of the short walls was curved. Like I usually do whenever I see new construction, I began to guess what it could be. Since it was the middle of the campus, I was sure it wasn't an Arby's or McDonald's. Once the block walls were completed I could see a big door on one side and another on the other. My best guess, I thought, was a bathroom. It reminded me of the kind you see at rest stops on the interstate. Why not a bathroom? Right here in the middle of campus? I had settled into my guess and was about to begin sharing this notion with others. That is, until one day a crew with a crane placed a shiny silver dome on top—a dome much like the one that crowns Monticello, the home of our fourth President of the United States. You can see a likeness of it on the back of some nickels. If it was a bathroom, you could sure store a lot of toilet paper in that thing.

Then one day in my campus e-mail I got a note that explained the construction: it's an observatory—for gazing at star clusters and galaxies and comets. I did a bit of research and discovered that the dome will house a 16" Schmidt-Cassegrain telescope. This meant nothing to me—but suddenly I wanted to look through it badly. I wanted to squint one eye and press the other to the lens and see everything up close: the moon, Jupiter, Saturn, Mars. I wanted to see the craggy surfaces on what looks like a simple pin-point of light in the sky. Stars of the firmament,

I've heard them called. I wanted to discover new galaxies, find stars, track asteroids that might be coming our way to destroy us. I wanted to see the heavens up close.

And this wasn't the first time I'd wanted that either. About five years before my wife and kids gave me a telescope for Christmas because I was itching with that same desire. The picture on the box had a photo of Saturn and Jupiter and a big misty, pinkish-looking glob identified as a crab nebulae. I set up my new telescope that first cold, December night in the backyard because I had to see Saturn right away. I wanted it to take my breath away. After working with the simple sky chart that came with the scope, I found it. And all the cartoons I'd ever seen about Saturn had gotten it right. Beautifully shaped circles ringed the white hot planet. The night air was below freezing, but the kids wanted to see too. So I focused on the accessorized planet while the kids waited at the back door. "Here it is!" I said. "Come see!" Zach raced out first and bent over the lens and made that squinty look that pulled one side of his face up into a snarl. "I don't see nothing," he said.

"It's there," I assured him. "Keep looking." After a few seconds of not seeing "nothing," and Chera over his back saying, "Let me see, let me see," Zach swung the telescope back and forth, exploring all of the heavens for a simple glimpse of Saturn's jewelry.

"Nope. Nothing." He backed away, hands up, obviously disappointed in my Christmas present. I tried again several times that night, finally figuring out that the rotation of the Earth is very, very fast. So fast, that if I focus on Saturn, I've got no more than ten seconds before it slides out of view before I have to find it again. There's a way to set it to automatically track with the earth's rotation, but I'd been in a hurry to see the stars, and there were some instructions to read. So the kids took turns: they'd crouch in a sprinting position just inside the door, racing out on my cue, then race back in when Saturn turned to "nothing." The joy on their faces was as warm as a comet. The joy on my face froze there because it was December and below freezing.

I've never been able to see the crab nebula with my telescope. But seeing this observatory, and its shiny chrome top with a slotted door that must slide open to make room for this 16" Schmidt-Cassegrain telescope that's inside, made me want to look at the heavens again. I wanted to be close enough to some stars—any stars—that I might believe I could reach out and touch them.

I passed by the new construction and entered my building where, taped to the wall, along with an advertisement for a rock group called Pop Vulture playing at Tomato Tomato, hung a notice for a Star Gazing Party on the last Friday of each month. I imagined loud music and finger foods and maybe a star-shaped piñata out on the grassy lawn. The next one was only two weeks away so I marked it in my planner. This flyer promised a special night because of the guest speakers, a husband and wife team: he's a cosmologist and his Website says he has a PhD in "relativistic quantum field theory and in cosmology and particle astrophysics." I didn't have a clue what that meant either, but my guess was that he knew how to use that 16" Schmidt-Cassegrain telescope. His wife is a philosopher and a writer—just like me (only without all that philosophy stuff). I was looking forward to the night, to a night where politics and religion were set aside and we could just gaze to the heavens and contemplate infinity.

Zach was eighteen and he and his buddy, Josh, had been hanging around the house that Friday afternoon—playing video games mostly. I told them about the Star Gazing Party and they must have been thinking hot wings and pizza because they agreed to go, but only if Zach could drive separately. That way if the night swung to boring, he and Josh could skedaddle. That was fine with me. I told them about the cosmologist who was going to be there, and Josh told me he had an aunt who does that. I was curious because I didn't know that about his family. "Yeah, she's done makeup and hair for years," he told me.

I met them at Wiser-Patten Science Hall. Above the entrance of the old building, carved in stone, is the single word "SCIENCE." Curved concrete steps were cracked and covered in a patina of old moss and rust. We entered and followed the signs to a worn granite staircase at one end of the hall that led down. Each step was cupped in the center because of the millions of footfalls over the years. The stairs reminded me of the stairs in the novel *A Separate Peace* by John Knowles, which has to be the best description of a set of stairs of all time. And I recalled the reason for the lengthy description is only because in that story someone falls on them and dies. I thought of this as we descended into the basement of the science building, our feet adding to the cupping of the granite steps. Remembering the novel, I used the handrail.

The lecture hall was laid out in theater-style seating for at least two hundred, but only thirty-seven people showed up for this special night. Josh, Zach, and I walked in during the introduction. We climbed some steep steps and found some seats about a third of the way from the top. A science professor—most likely an astronomer (tall, lean, dark brown hair combed to the side, Clark-Kent glasses, and a red windbreaker)—told the thirty-seven of us, spread to all quadrants of this large room, that our guest has "done it all." He told us that he's studied at universities around the world, with astronomers around the world, with cosmologists from around the world. I almost leaned over to ask Josh if his aunt ever worked with him, but remembered that sound carried in this old room. "And since we have heavy cloud coverage," our astronomer said, "we won't be able to view tonight. It'll all be lecture." I saw Zach squirm and heard him groan. But I was sure it wasn't the first groan ever heard in this room.

Our speaker stood up from the front row. He was shorter than the man who'd introduced him, heavier and older. His gray hair was combed over neatly and he wore wire-rimmed glasses. I marveled at what those eyes must have seen, given all the observatories he's had access to over the years. He'd probably seen crab nebulae until he was sick of them.

He began by explaining that since this was his fourth lecture in two days, he'd like to open the floor for questions. A student close to the front raised his hand. "How has this current administration harmed the national astronomy program?" Great, I thought. Politics. Our guest took a deep breath and told us that the Bush Administration has been the worst administration in history for the state of astronomy. He continued to tell us all that the Bush administration had screwed up, messed up, tangled up, diced up, minced up, and fouled up. I wanted to walk away because I hadn't come to hear a political trashing of the president. (I could get that pretty much any day on campus.) But I didn't want to cause a scene. Thirty minutes later that same student asked a follow-up question: "How well have the Democrats done since they got control of congress?"

"None," he said. "They're just as bad. Next question."

A young woman sitting close to the young man who'd asked the political question raised her hand and asked, "How difficult do you find it to do your work with cosmology under the pressure of the religious community."

Great. Religion. I wanted to raise my hand and ask if he could at least draw a picture of Saturn's rings on the board.

The Great Cosmologist (and political pundit extraordinaire) waved a short, dark-haired woman up from the front row and said, "I'm going to let my wife answer that one."

She took the microphone and, for a long time, she smiled before saying, "People turn to religion when they want to feel good about themselves."

Beside me Zach groaned like old lumber.

The philosopher/writer/wife told us that religion can make you feel good, but has no place in the study of the heavens. She said that for centuries people have operated under the strategy that if you don't believe like I believe, you're wrong. "We need a commonality," she said. "Something we can all connect with."

Like God, I thought, as I doodled in the margins of my notes.

"Each one of us," the soft-spoken philosopher continued, "is created from stardust." There was an awkward pause—even from the secular students who probably thought the Big Bang Theory was the greatest piece of science of all time. "Stardust," she repeated. I thought of an old Carpenter's song. The philosopher shook both arms before her in a rag doll sort of way, as if to demonstrate how stardust collected to form her arms. She swung one stardust arm—the one connected to the stardust hand that held the microphone—up to her mouth and said, "How awesome is that?"

I glanced over at the boys. Josh's eyes had glazed over. Zach looked startled, like teenagers will look sometimes when they hear a grownup say something that borders on ridiculous. I was thankful at this moment that he didn't know of the Carpenters.

But she did have a point. I thought that maybe she could still be leading to the creation story. You know the one, where God creates man out of the dust of the earth. It could still work. She tried to explain, again in another convoluted way, about how all that stardust was able to coalesce and grow legs and eventually build computers. And then she said, "I mean, when Mike Huckabee stood up there in front of everyone and said he did not believe in evolution . . ." Now she placed a hand against the side of her face, mouth agape in shock. ". . . how *embarrassing* was that?"

Zach leaned in so close to me that he bumped my shoulder. I turned and his face was only inches from mine. No stardust there. "Okay," he said, "I'm outta' here." Before I could say anything, Zach popped up. He's about five-foot-ten. Josh popped up too. He's about six-foot-three—and had a trucker's key chain that looped off his belt and jingled when he walked. Down the steep steps they went. Josh also wore boots that were a bit clunky. The mild-mannered philosopher continued to address the struggles between cosmology and religion—to present to this audience a cosmos where there is no God. I sat quietly, looking up from retracing some of my doodles, to watch my son blaze a trail down the center of the room, like a comet, with his tall friend trailing behind, clunking and jangling. The door was one of those double metal doors with the crash bar across the middle that's supposed to make it easier to open if you're in a hurry. None of them are ever quietly operated. When they reached the door, Zach didn't slow down. He crashed straight through. The door slammed shut behind him and the quiet-spoken woman was not fazed in the least. I imagined Zach and Josh on the other side, ascending the cupped steps, walking out into a cold night beneath a sky that was shielded for the moment by a veil of clouds. Even though they were quite loud when they walked, I was very proud of them.

I stayed until she finished, mostly doodling and wondering how anyone could live a life so close to the heavens and be content to believe the firmament is not miracle but only accident—no more miraculous than slipping down the steps.

As the night wrapped up I noticed that I had doodled several five-pointed stars in the margins of my notes. Crush them up, I thought, and toss the dust to the winds, and there's a good chance some people could pop up.

But since that wasn't likely to happen, I really wished we could have looked through that 16" Schmidt-Cassegrain telescope that night. That would have made me feel alive.

⁓

But I wanna feel something
Something that's a real something
That moves me, that proves to me I'm still alive.

—Trace Adkins, Country Music artist

⁓

2

(Not) A Way with Words

Back when I was alive, I didn't do very well with confrontation (not that I'm an expert now). For instance, the time a man with a knife came at me in the middle of the street—in the middle of the night. Rather than taking a stand or disarming him by means of a kick or punch or a Karate chop I could have only learned on TV, I depended more on my rhetoric—a self-consciousness of ominous vowels and harsh consonants. Lucky for me the drunk man couldn't open the pocketknife before our driver could stop laughing enough to punch the gas.

That driver would be my future wife, Chonda. At that time we were eighteen years old and good friends and had been on a mission most of the day to buy the perfect pair of dance shoes. She and I and her sister Cheralyn (who was sleeping in the backseat at the time of the knife attack) were in our high school musical *Oklahoma!* In that play is a dream sequence where the dream versions of the main characters perform a ballet-like dance: that was Cheralyn and me. So we found these dance shoes at a mall in Nashville and then had about a thirty-mile drive back to Ashland City. It was late and dark and, like I said, Chonda was driving because it was her car—an old (even then) Rambler. She was not proud of that car, even though the two of us had ridden a Greyhound bus all night a few weeks earlier to Cincinnati to pick it up from her father. On the way back we stopped seventeen times to fill it up with water. Once we made it back we were finally able to replace the bad hoses to end the water leak, but that didn't stop the fact that it was a big, white clunker (back then we just had to deal with our clunkers).

So we were nearly back to Ashland City when a giant truck passed us on the narrow two-lane highway. *Whoosh!*

"I think that was Kevin!" I said, loud enough to be heard above the roar of the Rambler. Kevin was Chonda's old boyfriend. I wasn't her new one yet, but I was on my way.

Maybe because Chonda wanted me to be her new boyfriend was why she did what she did next. "I'll show him," she said. And with that she gunned the rattling Rambler and on the first straight stretch overtook the giant pickup and passed him—just like that! Even though I was so close to the truck's driver-side window as we careened past, I still couldn't see inside the cab because it was dark and the glass glared. But I was pretty sure it was Kevin, and his truck. Chonda gave a yelp and I eased back into my seat. Just then Cheralyn woke up and raised her head above the backseat. "What's going on?" she said.

"That's Kevin behind us," Chonda said. "He passed us and we just passed him."

Just then the truck's headlights switched to bright and flooded our back window. I looked back and could make out Cheralyn's silhouette, but otherwise was pretty much blinded. Give it a rest, Kevin, I thought. But the giant truck and its high-wattage bulbs veered out and blew past us on the next straight stretch.

"Yeah, that's Kevin, alright," Chonda said, like she knew him based solely on his driving style. Just then, as her positive assertion still hung in the interior of the Rambler, the truck slammed on its brakes and came to a screeching stop angled in the middle of the highway. Chonda slowed and stopped too. A large man, bigger than the Kevin we knew, stepped out of the truck and into the lights of our Rambler. He staggered forward about two steps and then pulled something from his pocket. That definitely wasn't Kevin. It had been an honest mistake. I rolled down my window and hung out at least to my waist, ready to correct the mistake we'd made.

"Hey, buddy," I said. (To this day Chonda will tell you that I called him "friend." I did no such thing. *Buddy* has those two harsh consonant sounds in the *b* and *d* and that short *u* vowel is somewhat guttural. *Buddy* is a power word, with the power to affirm or condescend. *Friend* is too weak: the soft *f*, the purring *r*, the impotent short *e*. I would have *never*, especially in the life-threatening situation that we had found ourselves in, said *friend*.) "We thought you were someone else," I finished.

"You don't think I'll cut-*chu*?" he said, all slurry-like. He staggered closer, splitting our high beams with his corporeal self. I still hadn't seen the reflection of our high-beams off the blade yet because he still hadn't opened the knife. "I'll cut-*chu*!" He said this many times. Always phonetically consistent.

"Now wait a minute, *buddy*," I repeated, making sure to grate the intimidating consonants and gargle the guttural vowel. I turned to Chonda. She was laughing. Cheralyn reminded us from the backseat that this wasn't Kevin. "Just drive, Chonda," I said. She pounded the wheel and tried to catch her breath. In the meantime I was exposed waist up to a drunken, angry man who sooner-or-later would get that knife open. My only hope was that his fumbling would lead him to the can opener first. "Drive! Now!"

33

Chonda fiddled with the gear lever. I turned to the zombie-like man who staggered my way, chanting "I'll cut-*chu*!" and moving the pocketknife closer and then farther from his eyes as if he were trying to read small print. What he was doing was searching for the groove on the cutting blade so he could get a thumbnail in it to pull it open—and then cut me. Maybe he would never be able to figure out that pocketknife. He bent over and held the weapon in the high beams of the Rambler. "I'll cut-*chu*," he repeated. "You don't think I'll cut-*chu*?"

"Drive!"

Chonda found reverse and backed up enough to clear us from the man with the knife and then gunned the Rambler and we rumbled on down the highway, leaving Cutting Man in the dark.

"Friend?" she queried. And I understood right then what was happening. Chonda would never fully appreciate what I had just pulled off with only the power of selective consonants in conjunction with that perfect vowel. Rhetoric was lost on her, like water through a leaky Rambler.

I slumped into my seat, wondering how close to death-by-pocketknife I'd actually come. I could not explain to her then my overall strategy, the boundless, endless power rhetoric can have over sharpened steel (providing there had been a steel blade on that pocketknife at all). Weakly, spent of all rhetorical power now, I simply said, "I called him *buddy*."

"No, you didn't."

"Yes, I did." And I emphasized the finality of the *d*'s in *did* as well as that dart-like sound of the short *i*.

As passing air roared around the Rambler, as Cheralyn reminded us from the backseat that that had not been Kevin and asked what that was he'd been fumbling with and "Was he drunk?" I realized that this "Buddy" versus "Friend" argument could be a rub between Chonda and me for however long we might know each other. Thankfully, neither of us brought it up on our wedding day.

Thirty years later I still contend I said *buddy*. She'll say *friend*, using that ever-so- soft *f*, and she'll even over-do that rounded, smooth, musical *r*.

My goodness! Can she not see that every time she utters that word she only helps to prove my argument? Why would I ever call a man coming at me with a knife a *friend*? Give me a hundred knife assailants and I will refer to each and every one of them (drunk or not), and every single time, as *buddy*.

As a zombie, I found myself one day cheering and jumping from the sidelines of a college football game one moment and having one of those awkward, clumsy confrontational moments the next, where my rhetoric failed me badly and I could have used a little brawn against the short-bearded man with a monopod (a single-legged support used to steady a hand-held camera).

I had a good friend named Luke who worked for the Vanderbilt Commodores in Nashville and every home game he had a ticket waiting for me—a sideline pass. There's nothing that compares to walking the sidelines of a major college football game and making eye contact with people who are really supposed to be there. Some, I could tell, would see me and then privately wonder where they had seen me before. Whose son or father was I? Was I someone important? Someone they should be nice to? No one ever realized (as far as I could tell) that I was the heat and air conditioning guy on campus who went to high school with the assistant equipment manager. Once I even parked underneath the Tennessee Vols stadium in my Chevette—took a spot reserved for one of the Vanderbilt coaches and heard later that whoever he was he'd been extremely vile about not having a parking space. That was the year Tennessee won the conference and tore down the goal post and I was nearly trampled in the end zone. Fortunately I did a fake step to the right and juked back to the left and the fifty-three people carrying the goal post veered right, all team-like, and all was okay. Other times I brushed shoulders with Emmett Smith (who was on crutches at the time), Vinny Testeverde, Boomer Esiason, and Hershel Walker. And when basketball season came around I got pretty close up to Shaquille O'Neil and Charles "Bread Truck" Barkley (but basketball's a different story).

This particular game Vanderbilt was playing Florida. We (Vandy) hadn't beaten Florida in like a hundred years. But their star running back, Emmett Smith, was on crutches that day, so, like the mentality of most perennial-losing teams, because the best player from the other side was injured, we felt we had a shot that day. And we did.

On one particular play our running back (not a star, not a draft pick, and probably doing something like selling mutual funds today) broke loose and gained at least thirty yards down the sidelines—the one I stood on and paced with the fervency of a head coach. There were usually quite a few non-players on the sidelines. (If an assistant equipment manager can get four of his buddies on the sidelines, imagine how many others could be there!) So when our running back broke for a big gain, the guy in front of the guy in front of me stepped up to watch the play, which meant the guy directly in front of me stepped up, which meant I had to step up even farther to see around him. It was something like a domino effect only people didn't fall down, they just took one extra step forward until the last of the "lookers" was about ten yards onto the field, but far enough away from where the "action" of the play was taking place. After the play we'd always scoot back behind the lime line to keep everything legal.

But this was a big break-away run. We were Vanderbilt beating Florida. Emmett Smith was on crutches. We had a chance! So our guy broke loose and he was deep into Florida territory, and we on the sidelines did what we always did: stepped out, looked around the guy in front of us. If you had to go ten yards out onto the field, then you went. You could scoot back later.

So I did. I wasn't anywhere near ten yards out, maybe only three, cheering, yelping, feeling alive and—and there came a *tap, tap, tapping* on my lower leg. What was that? The roar of more than 40,000 still hung in the air when I looked back and saw a short man with a big camera fastened to a monopod. He wore a short scrubby beard and a scowl on his face. He wasn't looking at me in the eyes, but rather he was focused on my lower legs, at the point where he continued to rap me with that monopod of his. He was working it like he would a big stick to keep chickens from crossing over into a patch of grass you were trying to protect from their pecking. *Rap. Rap. Rap.*

I didn't move. The rapping didn't hurt, only irritated me—but that was fastly mutating, Hulk-like, into something else that made me fearful. *Rap. Rap. Rap.* I was waiting for his eyes to rise up and meet mine. Because the roar of more than 40,000 still hung in the air, I would need the benefit of lip reading for him to understand how I felt about his rap-rap-rapping at my lower leg.

Finally, he raised his eyes and rather than shocked or embarrassed, as I believed he should have been, he simply adjusted himself by pulling back the monopod, shrugged his shoulders, and then reset the monopod back into the sod so he could settle back behind the lens. Before he disappeared behind the camera, though, he told me, without a shred of politeness (all I needed was a smile or a shrug that I could interpret as "Hey, just trying to do my job, *friend*), he said, "Step back!" (exclamation mark his). He might as well have come after me with a pocketknife.

"Hey!" I called back above the din of more than 40,000, believing he wouldn't have any trouble reading my lips on that one. He stood rigid, his monopod out of the soil and hovering just above the grass, making small circles—a coiling, snake-like motion—awaiting to hear what I would say, see what I would do. I pointed at his monopod and exclaimed—feeling angry, violated, and empowered all at once—"Don't hit me with that." I took in what it was that he had rapped me with. The word I'd first chosen—tripod—no longer applied, but the crowd, the feeling of being violated, the short man with a scowl, the fact that we could beat Florida. I don't know which it was or what combination, if any, was at play, but I could not find the proper word.

And that in itself added to my overall panic. I tried again: ". . . that . . . that. . . ." The bearded man hung on patiently, and for the life of me I still could not think of what that *thing* was! The bearded, scowling man canted his head in anticipation. A tripod had three legs. But what was that "thing" when there was only one? I mentally scanned my foreign languages, which consisted mostly of one to ten in Spanish and one to four in French (I'd lost five through ten long ago), and hello in French, Spanish, Japanese, and Hawaiian. I knew I'd never heard of uno-pod before, nor un-pod. The crowd still roared, the short man still scowled, and the monopod still hovered. We might have even scored a touchdown, I didn't know. I pointed at the monopod and told the short, scowling man with a beard, "Don't hit me with that . . . *thing!*" Then I turned and stepped out onto the field, ten yards at least, to see if we'd scored. The man with the camera on the monopod backed away.

Soon the referees were herding us all back behind the lime. The man with the monopod was close by, but far enough away he couldn't reach me. His choice, I believed.

Later Luke asked me what it was that guy had said to me. "Which guy?" I asked.

"The one with the monopod," he said.

I wanted to hug Luke, but that wouldn't be appropriate. Unless we beat Florida, of course, then we could hug anyone for however long we wanted, and smack each other on the bottom too. "Just being a jerk," I said, while silently repeating the word *monopod* over and over again, so as not to lose it just in case I would need it later.

"Well, let me know if he bothers you again. I'll have him thrown out. Just say the word."

Monopod, monopod, monopod. "Thanks," I said. "Don't worry, I will."

It's good to be buddies with the assistant equipment manager. It made me feel alive.

I want to wake up kicking and screaming
I want a heart that I know is beating,
It's beating,
I'm bleeding.

—Switchfoot, contemporary Christian band

3

Life (and Its Evidence) Always Flows Downhill

Back when I was alive, I always believed my dad was the strongest man in the world. He had this thing he would do with a sledgehammer that would always make my brother and sister and me scream or hide our eyes or beg him to stop—sometimes all three. He'd grip the hammer at the end of its long handle and hold it up in front of him, arm extended. Then he'd slowly lower the head of the hammer in the direction of his own head until that mass of metal used for clobbering was only an inch from his nose. Then he would slowly raise the head of the hammer back up, lower it to the ground, and then look to us—for the applause he knew he'd receive. Dad would have made a great strong man in the circus.

Then there came a time when dad showed off his brains and I came to believe not only was he the strongest man in the world, but also a genius. We'd just moved from the hustle-bustle city life of Nashville to a little house out in the country—so far out in the country that we had no running water. There was, however, a beautiful spring about twenty feet away that bubbled up cold, clear water and was home to a giant crawdad that we'd get a peek at every now and then. For a few months Dad would dip out bucketfuls of water and bring them in and we'd dip out cupfuls for whatever we needed. Baths were not easy to do.

One weekend he brought the plumbing indoors. He drove up into the yard with a truckload of plastic and porcelain: PVC piping, a pump, a bathtub, a toilet, and a kitchen sink. He sank the pump next to the crawdad and cut and glued enough pipe to reach the house and connect it to where he'd set the new fixtures. I helped by dragging pipe off the truck and dabbing on glue after he'd point to the right spot. And just when I thought we were finished, Dad pointed out, in an almost professorial kind of way, that we had to get the water *out* of the house some way. So he drove back to the store for more pipe and glue. We fastened threaded fittings and glued elbows and 45-degree bends to all the drains and steered all the small lines to one big line that we ran through a hole we'd punched in the foundation. From there the idea was to lead the old water far away from the house—to the *other* side of the house from where the spring was. And to help us move it even farther from the house, we ended the pipe at the edge of a stream and hoped nature's flow would wash it far, far away. Because of Dad's genius, he made sure the water going out was downstream from the fresh water coming in.

That first flush was like witnessing a miracle. More than once I'd been outside playing when I'd hear a loud gurgle. I would stop whatever it was I was doing—stop in mid-play—just to catch a glimpse of the white plastic pipe shaking and blasting out something that should be far, far from the house. So cool. So ingenious.

This was only something I could marvel at for years—life flowing in, evidence of life flowing out.

Yeah, I was alive then. Very much so.

———————

As a zombie, I had to circle the block a few times before I could find the little house that was almost finished. Habitat for Humanity called it #85. Over the years they'd already built eighty-four houses in this area for families who'd probably thought they'd died and gone to heaven. I wanted the experience of helping someone feel like that. I'd called too late to get in on the early stages of this construction. I was hoping to use a hammer that day, or, better yet, a nail gun. I'd used one years before and that is still one of my happier memories. But all the nailing had been finished. Today I would use a razor—one already stained by another man's blood.

I took Zachary with me and his good friend Josh. I wanted them to experience the importance of volunteering too. To experience the overwhelming reward of helping a stranger. I found the house. There were a couple of trucks parked out front and the yard was still uneven and void of grass. The walkway to the front steps was framed with two-by-fours that had helped to shape the concrete, and probably only a few hours before, because it was still a dark gray that almost looked wet. The woman from the Habitat office had told me that this house was almost complete and so Zach, Josh, and I were the only volunteers there that day—except for the man who staggered out the front door, holding one arm up, squeezing his raised hand with his other. A ribbon of blood curled around his bare forearm, flowing to his elbow.

"I'm pretty sure it's going to need stitches," the bloody man said to another man who trailed him out the door.

"Let me take a look."

The wounded man stopped and lowered his hand. Then both men leaned over the naked wound as the injured one slowly pulled away the hand that stemmed the bleeding. The unwounded man must have gotten a good look because he pulled back quickly. The wounded man groaned, reapplied the pressure, and raised the injured hand back high into the air.

"Oh yes," said the unwounded man. "Get in my truck and I'll take you to the hospital." The injured man staggered off, zombie-like. The other man turned to us and said, "You guys here to work?"

I nodded. "You Terry?" I asked. The woman from the office had said to ask for Terry.

He nodded. He seemed to be sizing us up. He glanced at the house, then back to us. "What kind of skills do you have?"

"I've done a little bit of everything," I told him. "Heating and air conditioning, electrical, plumbing, you know, PVC work—water in, water out kind of stuff."

Josh said, "I can paint."

Zach said, "I can help my dad."

Terry thought for a moment and finally said, "There's a door casing on a closet in there that's got to come off. It's been painted already, so you'll have to take a razor and slice the paint around the frame so you don't tear the drywall." Then he looked at me when he asked, "Can you do that?"

I peeked into the open front door. Just inside I saw a closet door partly opened. On the floor was a box cutter.

"Is that what that man was doing when he almost cut off his hand?"

Terry nodded. "Yeah, I guess I'd better get him to the emergency room. You guys get started and I'll be back in a little bit."

Once Terry and the man who needed stitches drove away in the pickup truck, Josh, Zach, and I followed the blood trail to the closet— hard evidence of life flowing out.

David W. Pierce

*If a man does not make new acquaintance as he advances
through life, he will soon find himself left alone. A man, Sir,
should keep his friendship in constant repair.*

—Samuel Johnson (1709 - 1784), British lexicographer

*We sometimes encounter people, even perfect strangers,
who begin to interest us at first sight, somehow suddenly,
all at once, before a word has been spoken.*

—Fyodor Dostoevsky

4

The Life Raft(s)

Back when I was alive, I had a best friend named Bobby Felts. We were sixteen and had just started to drive, though neither of us had cars of our own. We lived on this skinny, crooked road that followed a river. There was always something to do along the river—like fish and swim at the least. The river fed into a shallow lake that rose and dropped with the level of the river. Sometimes, when the water was low, you could see big muddy islands in the middle of this lake. One winter the whole lake froze solid, and in Tennessee that is a big deal. So Bobby and I decided it would be fun to take our bikes out onto the ice. We'd spin the tires, slide left and right, and if we happened to find some traction, take off like a shot and then wipeout on purpose to send our bikes and ourselves into a crazy spin that would usually take us halfway across the lake. People would drive by and shout out to us from their rolled down windows just how dangerous it was—this bicycle-on-ice act that we were performing. We'd wave back politely, smile, and then have a good laugh together.

Later that summer, when we turned sixteen, we decided we'd build a raft—not because either of us had read Huck Finn, or because either of us knew the first thing about construction. Mainly, we decided to build a raft because we had time, some scrap lumber, and a river. We borrowed some tools from the owner of a convenience market nearby. We scavenged the banks for boards and found a lot of things had been deposited into the weeds and among the trees by one-time high waters. We found old logs, the bark peeled by time and weather and now smooth as stone. We laid them out into the shape of a square until we ran out of logs and then we cut some fresh trees to finish out the square. We bought some nails because we realized early on that we'd need a lot of nails. Over the next few days we hammered boards into place, connecting the logs together, making the structure solid and as one. We worked long hours on the muddy bank of this river, fighting mosquitoes and gnats, earning blisters, and sometimes smashing a thumb. In the end, our project was mostly square—and extremely heavy.

We worked half a day inching it closer and closer to the water's edge. We earned more blisters and smashed our toes more than once— and more than one toe. When we finally wrestled one edge of the raft into the water, we heaved with everything left in us and the big, heavy thing slid in . . . and under. We never imagined it *wouldn't* float. It was made of wood, wood that had floated once before. We were sure because we'd found it in the tops of tall bushes. And the trees we'd cut were now logs that should float, right? Could three boxes of nails be the difference?

We left our raft there on the bottom of the river, maybe four feet under the water. But the next day we had an idea, we had a remedy: plastic milk jugs. Jugs float, right? So we scavenged the banks again, this time looking for milk jugs. And we raided the neighbors' trash cans. I even went home and poured four glasses of milk and filled the refrigerator with topless drinks and raced off with the jug. Some had no caps and were useless to us. And most often the odor was rancid, but we couldn't let that slow us down. Once we had our big pile of milk jugs, we began the task of pushing them under our sunken raft, which required us to wade in and swim down. But it wasn't very deep. We only had to take a deep breath and hold it long enough to lift an edge and push a jug under. It was surprisingly hard to push a jug more than three feet under the water. But this gave us hope that our plan would work.

And it did. Before long our raft was flush with the surface. After a few more jugs—much easier to install now—we could ride on the raft, all sitting up nice and proud. We were floating! We were buoyed by plastic and soured air.

We crafted paddles from more boards we found. We chopped up small trees to make poles so that we could push off the bottom in shallow areas. That summer we rode our raft along the back of the slow river and around the shallow lake that we'd ridden our bikes on only a few months earlier.

Every minute on our raft was another minute of freedom. Because we were escaping. Bobby didn't want to go home—to the fighting, to a step-father who would berate him, who would shout in his face, who would shout at Bobby's mother. And I didn't want to go to the house, where most likely my father was drinking, was drunk already. We didn't fish from the raft though, that would have been a likely thing to do. Mostly, we swam. There was a great freedom in being able to step off the side of our raft, feel the cool water rush over my ears, flood my scalp. Sometimes I would open my eyes and could only see the dark—black, if I went deep enough, dark green as I'd rise to the surface. And then I'd crawl upon to the warm, wooden deck, and lie on my back with my face to the sun, each nail head a little point of heat that I didn't mind. It was our raft, our world, our refuge, and our escape.

We swam a lot, but mostly we talked. About school, about the wrestling team we were on. About certain girls—like Demitria, Beth, Robin, Crystal, Karen, Heather, Sarah, and sometimes Connie. About cars—like the new Le Mans or the hip Celica. About the BeeGees. And ABBA. We spent many hours that summer, basking in the sun on our raft, talking about the lives we lived.

Sometimes people in boats would come by and they would say hello. More than once someone would tell us a story about how he had built a raft when he was a kid, but not as good as the one we had. One person told us we might be—or definitely were—illegal. "Yeah, you're supposed to have a permit for anything on the water," he said. After that we were always on guard. We had no plan if we ever got caught. We'd built the thing for floating, not a high-speed chase. But we did make sure we hid it every day. We found some low-hanging branches that just about made the raft disappear when we pulled it under. That's where we tied it off each day. There was no trail to the raft, no markers. The only way to find it was if you knew exactly where it was. We never lost our raft. Not until the summer was over and we couldn't go every day. Winter came on. The waters rose and took our raft away. I like to think it broke up and the river deposited boards and smooth logs all along its banks, up in the tops of bushes and in the forks of trees, and that for many summers after, young boys were salvaging pieces to build their own rafts. I just hoped they could figure out the milk jug thing.

Yeah, I was alive then. Very much so.

As a zombie, I set out to find a friend. Actually, my counselor wouldn't let me leave the office until I came up with a name, "One person," she said, "that you could sit with and talk to."

Yeah, I was seeing a counselor because I couldn't do this zombie-killing thing on my own. "About what?"

"Anything. Everything. Or *nothing*. Just someone you can be with so you're not alone."

It'd been a long time since I'd had a friend that I could talk to like that. I thought hard about this. I stared at the door. It's not like she was blockading me and I couldn't get out. I imagined if I made a run for it, she'd just let me go. But like she said, I'd still be alone. And she was charging by the hour.

"Ken Davis," I told her.

She smiled and nodded and made a note in her pad. "Good. So he's a good friend?"

I shrugged. "I think he could be. I can try." She seemed pleased with this progress and told me to set up a date with him right away. I wanted to tell her that guys don't talk like that, but I knew what she meant.

Not long ago my wife wrote in a book (*Laughing in the Dark*) about our family and how we put puzzles together. It was very funny, but also very telling about me: "Then there is my husband. He's a picture studier. He picks out the object he wants to work on in the picture on the puzzle box. Then he gathers all the pieces with their pertinent colors, shapes, and hues; scoops them in to a cereal bowl; and moves to the end of the table away from the rest of the family. There he begins to work on his own private puzzle—alone. . . . Maybe you're the loner type. You gather the pieces you think you're going to need and then hunker down at the end of the table, away from everyone else. Somehow you feel safe there. You don't have to be bothered by input. You don't have to coordinate with other puzzlers. You can simple work on your own part of the puzzle—alone. Sure, you may feel a sense of accomplishment when you're done, but what happens when it's time to interlock with the rest of the world? You think, I don't fit in. I'm not ready for the world—or maybe the world isn't ready for me." I'd laughed when I'd first read that description of me. Now it had taken on a different meaning. Now I was dead. But I wasn't always like this, I kept telling myself, remembering that summer on the raft. There's got to be a way out of this.

It took me a few days and I had to have the right elements (or puzzle pieces) in place. I couldn't just call Ken and say, "Hey, let's go hang out together and be best friends forever." So just at the right time someone gave me free tickets to see comedian and talk show host Craig Ferguson. I called Ken and set things up. We met at a restaurant a couple of hours before the show. It was a laid back place with dim lighting and eclectic music. Not many people were there. The host was an older man in a white ski sweater. "Just the two of you?" he asked. He pulled a couple of menus and turned to lead us to a table. Then he stopped and seemed to take great care with how he was going to pose this next question. "Will you two be sitting *adjacent*?" He tucked the menus under one arm and used both hands to signal what adjacent would look like: side by side. "Or *across* from each other?" And then he made a motion with his hands I interpreted to be the one-person-on-each-side-of-the-table gesture. This was not like asking if you'd prefer a table or a booth. I looked at Ken and he looked back at me. "*Across* from each other," I said, and Ken quickly agreed. I repeated myself, but in a much gruffer tone this time. I used the same hand signals the host in the ski sweater had just used, so as to prevent any misunderstanding. So he led us to a small, small table and placed the menus there across from each other.

The thing about not having a friend, or someone to talk to, when you finally get the opportunity, there's always the possibility of gushing. For the next hour I talked and Ken sat there and listened. That small table became my giant raft. I told him about my job, about my family. I confided about my marriage problems and the anxiety attacks I'd been having. We talked about everything but the Bee Gees. I told him about my death and that part of my cure—or resurrection, more accurately—would be this moment tonight. I wanted him to sign something, some sort of a "friend receipt" that I could take back to my counselor as proof of this night. I was afraid there for a moment that he would cry, and then I would have to hold him and the man with the ski sweater would silently move in and place us adjacent to each other.

After nearly two hours of talk and peppered salmon, what we needed next was comedy. We were late to the show and discovered that our tickets were nearly to the front row. For over an hour and a half we just laughed. Ken took notes so he could tell his wife later what he had seen. I thought that was a smart idea. When I told Chonda later what I had heard and seen, I kept forgetting the punch lines. So I made a note to call Ken later and borrow his notes from the night.

When we stepped out of the theater, the temperature was below freezing, which wouldn't have been so bad if we could have remembered where we'd parked. "I remember walking uphill from the garage," I said.

Ken's eyes lit up. "So let's head downhill and see if anything looks familiar." My new friend not only listens, but he's brilliant. We circled the block twice. We soon realized that there were numbers on the individual spaces, even bigger numbers posted on the walls to indicate the level, and the floors were even color-coded. But no specific number or color would come to either of us. It seemed our car had just disappeared. A half-hour later, and three more garages, we found the right one. Swerved into it accidentally actually. Neither of us complained. And upon seeing the car, we shared this incredible sense of relief and celebrated by laughing and grunting.

When Ken dropped me off down the road at the restaurant where I had parked, he said probably the most important thing of the night: "If you need to talk, call me anytime. And I'll call you sometime just to see how you're doing."

As he drove off, I took a deep breath of the cold night air, let it flood my ears and pour over my scalp, like river water, feeling somewhat alive again. Then, for the life of me, I tried to remember where *I* had parked.

⁓

While we try to teach our children all about life,

Our children teach us what life is all about.

—Angela Schwindt, a home-schooling mom

⁓

Children make you want to start life over.

—Muhammad Ali

⁓

5

Those Silly Little Games

Back when I was alive, my future brother-in-law, Michael, took me to this place where he had found something he said was very, very special. There was a small market on the corner just a couple of blocks from the campus where we were both attending college. In the back corner, next to the magazine rack, was a box as tall as I was, but wide as a doorway and just as thick. At first glance it appeared to be a small television built into a wooden cabinet. Two knobs dotted the front, just below the screen. Across the top was an oversized single word: PONG.

"This is the neatest game," Michael said, approaching the box with something like reverence.

"It's a game? How does it work?"

Michael fished a quarter from his pocket and dropped it into the slot. The screen came alive with bright, white, vertical lines. At the top of each corner was a zero.

"It's zero to zero," he said. Then he pushed the start button and hunkered down over his side of the screen, twisting the knob back and forth as if to warm it up. Immediately another vertical line appeared— just spit out in the middle of the screen and drifted slowly, horizontally, to Michael's side of the screen. He twisted the knob he gripped and a different vertical bar zipped from top to bottom and seemed to block the moving one. It made a little *boink*! sound and the smaller line bounced back into my direction. I saw what Michael had done and began to move my knob like he had. I found my "paddle" and I tracked the vertical ball, but I couldn't get to it like Michael had because it was bearing down for the corner and there was no way . . . *boink-boink! bloop!* That thing just caromed like a marble in a box and then disappeared into a hole in my side of the screen! The zero in Michael's corner changed to a one.

"Keep up with it!" Michael said. "I just scored a point. Concentrate." I did concentrate. We had three dollars of quarters between us. So for the next hour and a half, I yanked the knob in one direction then the other. I did rapid logarithms and calculus on the fly to determine the angle of reflection based on the immediate angle of incidence. My forearms began to ache, my thumbs turned raw. And the longer we played the faster that little hash mark moved. And my "paddle" hash mark began to shrink. "That's what makes it challenging," Michael said.

But since we were both college students, and Michael was married and living in the married students' apartments, we didn't have a lot of $3 days we could throw away like that. Thank goodness Michael bought the home version. After that we had "Pong Parties," which consisted of a bunch of us guys coming over and playing for hours. Here's what they sounded like: *boink! boink! boink! boink-boink! boink! boink! boink! boink! boink! boink! boink-boink! boink! boink! boink! BLOOP!* "YEA! All Right! Give me five!" The little apartment roared with the sounds of PONG—and humans.

And that was all for free. Yeah, I was alive back then. Very much so.

As a zombie, we got a new game in the house—Guitar Heroes. It'd actually been there awhile before I discovered it—right after Zachary downloaded a ton of songs from the '70s and '80s. I walked through the room the other day and Boston's "Long Time" was cranked up to about nine on a scale of ten. So I did what you're supposed to do: I pumped my fist in the air and started singing along. Zach hit the pause button and stared at me, nonplussed. "You know this song?" he asked.

"Know it?" I said. "I lived it! Now . . . un-pause it."

Shortly after that he handed me a guitar and we built a playlist with bands like Blue Oyster Cult, Bon Jovi, Allman Brothers, Molly Hatchet, and Lynyrd Skynyrd. (He let me play the guitar at the easy level while he played the drums at expert level.) Following the colored-coded notes and executing perfect timing to hit the button that is supposed to be the guitar strings is no easy task. Whenever I hit the wrong note, Zach would shake his head and tell me to concentrate harder. But concentrating harder only made me miss more notes.

How productive is Guitar Heroes anyway? At the end of an hour and a half of rocking out Detroit, all I had to show for it were sore wrists and burning eyes. A former lead singer of a big country group told me the other day that he thinks Guitar Heroes really does help with learning to play a real guitar. "It teaches timing and discipline," he said. I asked Zach if he wanted to learn to play a real guitar, and he said no. I asked him if he's learning timing and discipline, and he said no. What does my professional musician friend know anyway?

A few days after that, a meat salesman, who comes through the neighborhood every few months and sells me really good steaks at a fair price, told me that his other job is in a rock band. "Man," he told me. "That Guitar Heroes can make you look silly. I mean, man, I play lead guitar. I can do arpeggios and everything, man. But when I try to play that game, my fingers get all tangled up." He might have said "man" once or twice more. But I don't want to write that anymore. He played a bit on his air guitar to show me what that would look like. It was like he said, silly. (I looked up arpeggios later because I figured if a meat salesman who also plays in a rock band knows what it means, then I should too, man.)

My fear is that I'm wasting time banging on a piece of plastic. That I'm fastly contracting Carpel Tunnel Syndrome. That my son will never find a job that will require him to use his Guitar Heroes skills. I fear all these things—until my son hands me my plastic guitar the next day. Like always, there's a gleam in his eye, and a smile ready to break out. "Let's rock and roll, Dad," he says. I take the guitar and say, "Got any REO Speedwagon on there?" He shakes his head in amazement. "What'd you do growing up? Listen to music all the time?" Sure I did, I think. And I wish I could tell him that I listened to music with my dad *all the time*. But that wouldn't have been true. And, besides, it was time for my guitar solo.

Maybe the game does teach us timing and discipline. Or maybe it can only make us look silly. But last night Zach and I rocked a make-believe frat house for about an hour and a half. At the end of the set, he turned and gave me a high five. I wonder what he'll tell his children one day about this silly game. About the night we were both living large at Alpha Delta Pi, man.

David W. Pierce

—

And out of the darkness, the Zombie did call
True pain and suffering he brought to them all
Away ran the children to hide in their beds,
for fear that the devil would chop off their heads.

—"Call of the Zombie," a song by Rob Zombie

—

film director, musician, screenwriter

Passing stranger! You do not know how longingly
I look upon you,
You must be he I was seeking, or she I was seeking. . . .

—Walt Whitman, "To a Stranger"

—

6

Something a Little Less Dangerous, Please

Back when I was alive, Butch and I headed to Colorado to celebrate having graduated high school. The plan was to hitchhike there and back, but Butch's parents thought that was too dangerous, so we drove out in his Volkswagen Beetle and its four bald tires. It is a thousand miles from Nashville to Denver and we drove straight through—leaving Nashville at noon one day and arriving in Denver at noon the next. It's not easy sleeping in the passenger seat of a Beetle.

Butch was worried about the tires. "May-pops" is what he called them, because they may pop at any given time. He had a spare but no lug wrench, so we bought one at an auto supply store just outside Denver. Then we bought a cooler and filled it with meat and headed into the mountains. We had no plans at all. We figured we'd make a big circle for about a week and then head home because we were college men now and had to get started on our futures.

Every night we bought more meat and built a fire and ate off of dirty dishes. We usually rinsed them in a river, but we didn't have any soap. And we didn't have a tent either, just a tarp that we'd tie up to a tree and the side mirror of the Volkswagen. We drove through towns like Granby, Georgetown, Glenwood Springs, Leadville, Aspen, and Gunnison. Never once did we shower. Butch tried washing his hair once because it had become stiff. But it was a hurried job and not very thorough because the water was too cold to endure. One day we saw a naked man standing at the edge of a waterfall, soaped up from head to toe. Like I said, we chose not to bathe that week.

We spent half of one day in a garage. The Beetle had a real problem with vapor-locking. Someone explained it to us as we sat on the side of the road with our emergency flashers on. Because of the altitude the air was rather thin. Sometimes there wasn't enough air to mix with the fuel to create the proper combination for combustion. The cure? Sit and wait, the man told us. So we did that a lot on the mountain. It happened to us so much in fact that I told Butch that maybe it's the points. That's the problem. Back when cars had points. It's a simple part. Basically it's the part that sparks. There didn't seem to be a spark. So we told the guy at the garage that we (I) believed we need new points. He set out to replace the points. But because he was the only one working the little mountain garage, he was interrupted many times to pump fuel and clean windshields—back when garage attendants did that sort of work. Four hours later he told us we were ready.

"So you think that'll fix it?" Butch asked.

The mechanic shrugged and said, "You said you wanted points, I put in points."

"But that fixed the problem, right?"

The mechanic shrugged again.

We pooled our money together and paid the man $40. An hour later we were on the side of a mountain, waiting for the vapor lock to go away.

We were on our way back, passing through New Mexico when we were almost killed and Butch saved my life.

Our Beetle was the sickest yet. It sputtered and spit and could go no faster than thirty miles an hour. I was sure we could hitchhike faster than this. "It really acts like bad points," I said. Butch was driving and he ignored me. I was pressing against the dashboard, trying to make the car go faster. About ten that night we pulled into a tiny town where we hoped we might find a mechanic the next morning. It looked quaint enough until we got to the end of the street. There was a bar, festooned with neon. It seemed to be the only bar in town. And it seemed everyone in town was here. The front window was filled with people dancing, or at least jumping up and down. Loud music blared through the glass. "We'd better not go in there," Butch said and steered the sputtering Beetle to the outskirts of town. We didn't even tie the tarp up that night. We pulled the sleeping bags out and lay by the car and watched shooting stars until we fell to sleep. I awoke to the sounds of laughter, squealing tires, and breaking glass. I sat up straight when Butch grabbed my shoulder and pulled me back. "Shhhhh," he said, and for a moment I stopped breathing. I raised my head just enough to see a pickup truck close by loaded with a gang of drinking (and probably drunk) men, still jumping up and down like they had been in the window of the bar. The breaking glass was from bottles being thrown from the truck onto the street. They drove slowly by. Even our Beetle seemed to cower. We were invisible in the grass. Then the tires squealed and the truck raced away, leaving behind broken bottles and tossing back full-throated screams, and Butch and I lying in the grass, praying.

The next morning someone stopped to help us—someone who knew all about Volkswagens. "Let's see here," he said, adjusting his glasses and poking around at the carburetor. "Looks like you got a loose screw." (This may be the most truthful part of this whole story!) He tightened it with his fingers and said, "Try that." The car took off—sputterless! As we sped away, on our may-pop tires, I stuck my head out the window and waved a big thank you. I guess it wasn't the points after all.

Yeah, I was alive then. Very much so.

As a zombie, I was in Los Angeles one night because my wife, Chonda, was working. But she also liked to shop. When she shops I usually just hang. Watch. Wait. Sometimes I hold her purse. This night I'd decided I was going to talk to someone. I was going to initiate a conversation for the sole purpose of connecting with a fellow human being. Just make small talk, I told myself. No matter how uncomfortable, it's these connections that will quicken that sullen spirit of mine. At least I was buying into that idea for now.

Not too far away I spotted someone I wanted to talk to. I chose him mainly because he was the only man in the place at the time—the H&M store on Sunset Blvd, a woman's clothing shop. Already I imagined a kinship, a certain kind of fellowship that men in dress stores understand. Although he wasn't holding a purse, I believed he was as bored as I was. He was a big Hispanic guy. Over six foot. He was leaning forward with his elbows on a rack of dresses. His head was shaved and he wore wraparound shades. As I approached slightly from behind and to his right, I noticed that most of the back of his head was taken up in a tattoo. Just above his medulla obbligato were the capital letters "BH."

"Hey, dude," I called out when I thought I was close enough to be heard above the loud pop music playing in the store speakers. I never say "dude," but something in my gut told me this time it would be appropriate. He swiveled his head just enough to find me. I circled a hand over the back of my own head and asked him, "So what's the BH stand for?"

He kept his weight rested on the dress rack. I couldn't read his eyes for the shades, but the corners of his mouth were turned down. He said something, but I couldn't hear above the music. So I asked him again. He told me but I still didn't know what he'd said. Once again I listened to my gut that told me (begged me) not to ask for a third time. I nodded as if I'd heard. Then he added, "It was a gang I was in."

Even though I'm from Tennessee, I'd heard about LA gangs—just that there are gangs and sometimes they can be dangerous. But this guy was alone. No gang to back him up. I figured he didn't have to put on a tough-man show for me. Maybe that's why I was bold enough to ask him, "So what did you do in the gang?" (For the purpose of some potentially sensitive members of my audience, I will now censor the remainder of this story. If I do this well, you'll never know what words have been changed.)

He said, "Stupid sugar, mostly."

I nodded and said, "Hey, who doesn't?" He looked away from me, across racks filled with dresses, some up to 75% off. "So you're not in the gang now?" I asked. He scowled, and I was glad he was wearing the shades now. Kind of a what-I-don't-know-won't-hurt-me thinking, I guessed.

"I've been in prison most of my life." He was looking right at me now, or at least the shades were aimed right at me. "I'm on parole now," he said.

Heat rose up my neck. I'd registered the word *parole*. Back home when you asked someone what it is he did for a living, it's proper to repeat the occupation and then make a comment about it. If someone tells me he's a dentist, I say, "Wow, a dentist!" Then I try to think of my best dentist story, preferably something funny. I was thinking now how that is a stupid routine, but I couldn't stop myself. "Parole?" I said. "Wow, dude!" (Why am I saying dude all the time?) "And look at you now." I extended a hand toward him, palm up, waved it a bit. "You're out, and...." I had no funny parole stories. "...you're in a..." I looked around. I wanted to say something like *a place of freedom*. Something that would capture the notion of *fetterlessness*. Instead I said, "...you're in a dress shop."

His expression went stony (or stonier). This conversation was supposed to make me feel alive, not get me killed. Quickly I used the same story I used when I drive in a city I've never been to before and it seems everyone's blaring horns at me. I said, "Dude, I'm from out of town. This is my first time in LA. I'm from Tennessee."

The dude canted his head the slightest. His stoniness seemed to soften. For the first time he asked me a question: "Home of Elvis Presley?"

I pumped a fist in the air and said, "King of Rock'n Roll! Yeah, we claim him. He's ours." I brought my fist down because I didn't feel totally honest. "But I'm a big country music person myself."

Now the dude pushed back from the dress rack—yeah, he was over six foot—and said, "Country music?" I nodded. He took a breath-and-a-half and said, "Country music pretty much saved my life when I was in prison."

My soul stirred, totally in a genuine way. "Really?" I said.

He nodded now. "Yeah. Shania Twain. She's something."

We'd connected and I wanted to keep this going. But what do I say about Shania Twain? If I started singing "Man, I Feel Like a Woman," he might cut me with a shiv, so I thought. Then I said, "Can you believe *her* husband left *her*?"

He shook his head sadly and frowned and said, "Now that's some messed up sugar right there."

I nodded. "Absolutely."

"So let me get this straight. You come all the way from Tennessee to spend your money in LA?"

I shrugged. "If we didn't spend it here, we'd spend it there. Shopping, you know." He nodded and cut a slight glance back over the fiery-red clearance sale signs. Between country music and shopping with women, we'd connected. I saw Chonda in a nearby clearing. Her arms were full and I figured she'd need help pretty soon, so I told my new friend I guess I'd better go over and at least try to slow her down. I walked away and I heard him call out, "Hey, dude!" I turned around and he was giving me a crooked smile and one of those fist pumps in the air. "Welcome to LA!" I fist pumped right back and went to find my wife.

While on the plane to LA I finished reading *To Kill a Mockingbird*. The final thought of that book, articulated by an eight year old, still resonates with me: How can you ever know someone if you never see them? In this case, tattoos, shades, scowl, and crooked smile. I saw him—the LA Gang Dude.

Later, back at the hotel, I went to Google and did a search on "LA gangs BH." I got two options: either he was a member of the Bloodhounds, with an estimated four hundred kills over the past five years, or he was a member of the Booty Hunters. Either way I'm left with one sobering thought: *Hmmm, I wonder if his homeboys know that he's a country music fan?* If they did, they'd probably give him a lot of sugar about that.

~

Nobody heard him, the dead man,
But still he lay moaning:
I was much further out than you thought
And not waving but drowning.

—Stevie Smith, British poet

~

Breathing in and out's a blessing can't you see . . .
I'm alive and well.

—"Alive and Well," by Kenney Chesney and Dave Mathews,
country singer and pop singer, respectively

~

7

Me, My Buddies, and Death Take a Trip

Back when I was alive, I used to hang out with the boys and laugh in the face of death. I was in college and worked at an apartment building that was for senior citizens only. We'd planned a weekend camping trip for weeks. Eight of us, all twenty-somethings, were going to drive from Nashville to Cleveland, Tennessee, about thirty miles north of Chattanooga because that's where the Ocoee River is, a class five white-water river. A few years later this is where the 1996 Olympics in Atlanta would hold the kayaking competition. What better place to invite death into our raft, so we could laugh in its face?

Eight of us packed into an eight-man van loaded with gear. We set up camp that first night, grilled some burgers, and then giggled ourselves to sleep. First there were the stories, that led to the laughs, that led to the farts, that led to the giggles. Then the Park Ranger showed up and we went deathly quiet while he told us all how he could toss us out in a heartbeat. It didn't sound right to come limping home without having looked death in the face and having to explain how we got barred from our campsite for giggling.

Later that night the rains came in—no, a deluge—and we slowly began to learn how un-waterproof the tent was. Water worked its way into seams and onto pillows. A couple of the guys crawled out and scampered to the van. Water blew up sideways and at impossible angles to seep around the flaps. Three more of us raced for the van. Water puddled under the tent and with only three people left, threatened to wash it across the campsite and most likely into the nearby river. The last three of us packed into the van. Someone farted and everyone giggled. But there was no way the Park Ranger would come out in this stuff.

The next morning we drove to an address we had that promised to give us a tour down the river. We filed out of the van and into a little country store on the side of the highway. "Oh yeah," the older woman behind the counter said when we told her why we were there. "I'll have to call John. He's out farming this morning."

So we kicked around in the gravel parking lot until John showed up. He was a likable fellow, probably in his thirties, tanned and weathered, wearing overalls. He talked with a thick, country drawl. "If you boys'll help me with the raft, we'll load it up on the bus." They kept a giant raft, big enough for all of us, in a shed behind the market. We hoisted it over our heads and worked it upon the top of an old school bus that would take us upriver. John strapped the raft down and then drove us upstream. I worried that he had beans in a field that needed cultivating badly.

We followed a winding road that matched the crazy curves of the river. Only it wasn't much of a river. It was more like a bed of rocks and boulders with very little water in the bottom. "This is not the river," someone said, only it was more like a question to John.

John grinned as he steered the old bus with both hands. "Oh yeah," he said. "That's it. We should be meeting the water in just a little bit."

After another two miles he announced, "There it is!" We pressed our faces to the glass on the right side of the bus and witnessed a greenish-brown wall of water, white-capping and foaming and racing rapidly, tumbling down the rocky channel. On the backside of the tumbling wall the river was wide and wild-looking. A somber feeling seemed to settle over the bus. A specter capered about that no one was willing to address just yet. But we would get bolder.

John made us wear some helmets and life vests. And as far as training or practicing, he held up a paddle and said, "This is forward paddle." And he made a nice, simple stroke in the air to demonstrate. "And this is back paddle." Now he reversed the stroke. "Sometimes I might say, 'Right side, back paddle.' When I do, you back paddle like crazy. Same to you left side." We drug the raft to the river's edge. Misty sprays kicked up from the violent water. John had to talk louder here at the water's edge because it was so loud. "Now we have a few options here," he began. "With most every section, there is the safest way and there is a more dangerous option."

"Danger!" someone shouted.

"Yeah, danger!"

"Give us danger!"

"We laugh in the face of death!"

John the farmer grinned and then he proceeded to lead us down the path of danger.

The path of danger had such rapids named Table Saw, Diamond Cutter, Double Trouble, Broken Nose, and Hell Hole. Maybe John didn't trust our date with danger. Nearly every time before we began a new section he would start with, "Now if we go down the left side of this one, it'll be pretty safe or—"

"Danger!" someone would shout and we'd do it all over again. It was always our choice.

We stopped at a place just before Hell Hole to dump the water from our raft. Hell Hole had a history and a story that John chose to tell us about now, on the bank so that we could all see and hear him. There was a bridge that stretched across the river just downstream from us. Beyond that was a short falls, only three feet, but enough that it would be a good and "dangerous" ride, John explained with a grin. "Now keep in mind that even a little bit of a fall will create something known as hydraulics. Life vest or no life vest, hydraulics can hold you under water. So if we get tossed, hang on to the raft. Wedge a foot into the side. Hold on to the rope. You lose a paddle, we'll pick it up downstream. You just stay in the boat. Now first we want to get past the bridge pylon. Then when we hit Hell Hole we want to make sure we're nose first. We sure don't want to go sideways—not there."

We missed the bridge easy enough, but we hit Hell Hole in a perfect sideways position, like we shouldn't have. Someone yelled "Back paddle!" but I couldn't tell which side. Didn't matter anyway. The raft dipped down, into the hole of Hell Hole, then shot back up, straight into the air. Bodies went flying out. I lost my paddle and clutched the rope that threaded the outer rim of the raft. So did others. We drifted past the worst part and somehow everyone had hung on. We helped each other back into the raft. That's when we noticed Jeff wasn't there.

"Anyone see Jeff?"

"Jeff!" we took turns calling.

Cold settled into the raft. John's speech about hydraulics played in my mind. He was being held under. The hydraulics wouldn't let him go. We drifted and the raft spun lazily now, away from the water that churned in Hell Hole. Heads swiveled right and left. Eyes scanned the churning surface. We took turns calling out his name. We had chosen danger. Death had cozied up into our raft and no one wanted to look at it now.

When Jeff's head bobbed to the surface like a cork, he spat out a wide spray of river water. He coughed and spun himself about in the water, looking for us like we were looking for him. When he saw us he pumped a fist into the air and laughed. We pounded the raft and screamed and laughed and called Jeff's name out as if he were a hero. We dared the Park Ranger to toss us from this river for cheating death.

On the way home we joked about our adventure. Jeff had toed-the-line. We had come, bragging about how we laughed in the face of death. Death had responded with "Oh, really?" And we quietly and tacitly withdrew our giggle. Death rode back to Nashville with us, a big, cold reminder to be careful. To enjoy life for life's sake, not to taunt Death. What fun is that?

We rode home closer than eight men in an eight-man van had to be. We'd shared one another's fun and one another's fear. We shared each other's space.

Yeah, I was alive then. Very much so.

As a zombie, I sat on the edge of a boat. On the count of three we were to roll backward out of the boat and into the choppy water . . . because that was the best way to get out of this small dive boat and into the water with all the scuba gear on.

"One!" called out the dive master.

The technique is called a "roll out." I stuck my mouthpiece in and clamped it hard between my teeth.

"Two!"

But before we roll out, let me tell you who we are and how we got here—to Tobago, a small island just north of Trinidad and just northeast of Venezuela. In the harbor sits anchored Frank's Glass Bottomed Boat.

Ken Evans is the one who started my scuba diving career. He is the husband of my wife's best friend. Years ago we took a vacation together and since he doesn't play golf, I got certified to dive, because that's what he does. Over the years we've dived the caves (or Cenotes) in Cancun, swam with the sharks in the Bahamas, the sea lions and hammerhead sharks in the Sea of Cortez, the turtles in Kauai, and the barracuda in Panama. Ken likes to find these out-of-the way places, far from cruise ship tourists. This usually means we sleep in places like we did in Panama—at Manuel Noreiga's old haunt about twenty-five miles off the west coast on a small island in old army barracks and with a handful of guards with automatic weapons, who patrol the area for drug runners. In the bay behind the barracks lives an old crocodile they call Tito. We made sure to walk briskly to breakfast—especially if we couldn't see him. When we did see him, usually beached in the surf with birds boldly lighting on him as if he were a log, we'd toss old Vienna sausages to him and discuss a route of escape just in case he was emboldened to attack.

So Ken found this place on the north side of Tobago in a town called Speyside. This was another trip for the "boys." We have a core group of divers with combined hundreds of dives. Steve Roos alone has over seven hundred. (I'm closer to one hundred.) Steve's a giant. He's about my age but has at least a foot in height and a hundred pounds on me. He always runs point in the airports because we can spot him in crowds. We always give him the front seat in the taxi because of the extra leg room. And if I have an aisle seat and he doesn't, we change. And as if he didn't take up enough space, leave a big enough footprint, Steve likes to bring his cameras along. He packs them in two hard-shell cases that are a pain to get through security because of all the battery packs and wires and bulbs. I'm sure to the security people it's a camera that looks like a bomb, or a bomb that looks like a camera. As inconvenient as his trip through security might be, it's not as bad as the time we had one diver who had to bring along his own defilbulator—doctor's orders. It was worth hanging around just to watch the security guard's face as our friend tried to explain what it was for while he unbuttoned his shirt to show him his scars. Steve may be a big guy, but as Ken says, "Under water he's a ballerina."

Bill Davis is another in our group. Like Ken, he's a doctor, family practice. Bill moves at his own pace—slow—whether it's eating, packing, walking, or poking at an octopus in a hole, which I've seen him do more than once.

We breathe from forty-pound tanks that hold 3000 psi of compressed air with a finite number of breaths in each. The air is drawn through a rubber tubing a half inch in diameter, through a mouthpiece that I clench like pliers between my teeth. When I complained about a sore spot on my gum after day two, Bill said I was biting too hard. "Just relax. Hold it between your teeth easily." But I'm afraid if I relax too much the rubber mouthpiece will simply *phttttt!* right from my lips.

"Three!"

The four of us and our guide rolled back together. My tank made a *splat!* sound against the surface. I spun upside down but quickly turned upright, clenching the mouthpiece so hard that my teeth hurt. And I was holding my breath. When the wall of bubbles cleared I could see my friends through the murky water, and I remembered to breathe. Slowly and steadily, Darth Vader-like. We passed around the OK sign and then began to sink—forty, fifty, sixty feet—until we hovered just above the most incredible coral fields I'd ever seen. Whoever named the corals, however, didn't try to get too creative. My guess is that any attempt at creativity amidst the pallet of colors and shapes and textures we were witnessing would fall way short. Instead the coral has simple descriptive names like antler, sponge, fan, and brain. Any non-diver could easily figure out what these look like. We floated above one of the largest brain corals in the world, as big as a bus. I imagined for a moment it was a real brain. If so, it could possibly contain all the knowledge of the world—an underwater super computer. A yellow tang swam out of a hole in the side of the giant brain, and I wondered what sort of knowledge the little swimmer had picked away while he was in there.

A few moments later I spotted a pair of fire worms, at least eight inches long, crawling centipede-like from beneath a chunk of coral onto bone-white sand. I looked around to tell someone. I figured Steve would want to take a picture of them. Of course you can't talk under water. So I waved frantically, but no one was looking. I should have brought something to tap on my tank, I thought. That's what the dive master does when he wants to get our attention. For a moment I was frantic. I felt constricted and suddenly lonely there waving my arms, drowning in the silence. And worst of all, I had no one to share the fire worms with. So we drifted along—like you do under the ocean.

With each dive we usually stay down about fifty minutes before we make our way back to the boat. We'll take an hour break and then switch tanks and make another dive. On a good day we like to do two in the morning and two in the afternoon. On this trip we did nine dives—nine tanks. Steve, however, in the same way he needed extra leg room on the airplane, needed two tanks on each dive, or at least a tank and a half. Since I usually came up with 1,000 psi or more, I shared my air with Steve. I gave him my unused breaths. There was something about passing off those unused breaths each time that made me feel good, almost noble.

On our last night there we asked Andy, our cab driver, to join us for dinner. He told us of the time he lived in the United States, for twenty-six years. He was a steelworker in New Jersey and helped build the Times Warner Building on Columbus Circle in Manhattan, the one someone tries to climb like a spider every few months.

Steve said, "You ever drop anything?" If it was a silly question, we all leaned in anyway because we all wanted to know. I wanted to ask if he'd ever spit from the top.

"Yeah," Andy answered as he nodded. "Bolts, mostly. Dropped a lot of bolts."

And somehow, like conversations with strangers tend to go if they last long enough, he talked about death. "I saw a lot of men—good men—die on those high rises. I saw a man die when someone dropped a bolt and it hit him the top of the head. Went right through his hard hat." Andy paused and it seemed as if we'd decided to take a moment of silence for this dead man. "I saw another man step off the construction elevator. He was bringing coffee to some men. Usually a steel floor will drop down when the elevator opens." Andy used his hands to show us how that walkway should have dropped down. "But this time it didn't. It was cold, maybe it froze or something. He dropped about eight stories and landed like a book across the steel at the bottom. He was a good man."

We took another moment of silence. Andy took a deep breath and let out a what-can-you-do sigh. Bill nodded, slowly. Then Andy waved over a friend of his and introduced us to him. He was the owner of the restaurant, Frank—the same Frank who owned the glass-bottomed boat in the bay. We talked awhile about the glass-bottom boat business, about his restaurant, his hot sauce that singed the inside of my eardrums, about America, and about how Andy had met his wife and how Frank was building a new restaurant. There at Frank's we breathed in and out, drawing down our finite number of breaths one at a time. But we also did something that is most important, that is more urgent than capturing a collective look at a fire worm: we talked and listened. Underwater that's impossible and could lead to drowning. But at Frank's, when we could sit and eat fresh lobster and Wahoo, we relaxed as we breathed;

we shared one another's air and listened to stories about death—that only reminded us about life.

About a week after we returned from Tobago, I heard from Ken. He lives in a small town in South Carolina. His friend owns a small hardware and feed store that also sells ax handles. That day someone had come in and robbed the man, right after he beat him to death with one of the ax handles. I didn't even know the man, but the story broke my heart and then made me angry. I called Ken to see how he was doing. "It just doesn't make sense," he said. He might have even said that more than once. I know the words echoed in my head for a long time after that. That simple statement by Ken may be about as close as we can get to understanding why good people die such horrible deaths. And us trying to make sense of something so senseless can only frustrate. Sometimes there is nothing in the world we can do.

All the more reason for me, whenever I can, to be with friends and to share my breaths. To know I am alive.

David W. Pierce

~

After talking about his family, and promising his son
that one day he would bounce his kids on his knees, Tony
Snow began to weep. After a moment of this he said,
"It's great to love people this much."

—Tony Snow, former White House Press Secretary, July 12, 2008

~

8

Some Very "Live"-ly Crowds

Back when I was alive, eleven of my closest friends and I found a real haunted house. I was twenty and working as a maintenance man for a high-rise apartment building filled with retired folks, doing things like cleaning air conditioner filters, fixing leaky toilets, and unstopping the trash chute whenever someone would try to jam down a cardboard box without crushing it first—stuff like that.

Ron was the one who told us about the place just outside of Nashville. He'd found a story in the newspaper about an old abandoned house that had been empty for over sixty years—ever since the husband had murdered his whole family *with an ax!* He showed us the paper one morning before work began. We passed it around and as we silently read the who, what, when, where, why, the giddiness we briefly possessed that seems to come at the beginning of a good ghost story dried up, and a somber air settled on us. With the paper lying lifeless on the table before us, there in the cave-like basement of the high rise, Ron first broached the idea: "What do you say we go find it? Tonight?" No one cheered on the idea, but neither did one soul vote no.

So that chilly October night all eleven of us loaded up in the company van. (Since Ron's father owned the place, we could do stuff like take the company van out in the countryside to an old haunted house without getting into trouble.) This van, though, was meant for hauling stuff—lumber, plumbing parts, produce, people in wheelchairs—so there weren't any seats except for the two up front. Ron drove and Jerry got the passenger seat, since he was the biggest and seemed more like an adult than the rest of us. Jeff, Mike, Luke, Wendell, Tim and John, Jon, Jonathan, and I found a spot in the back on the hard steel flooring. It was a long drive, maybe forty-five minutes, so if you didn't readjust every so often, part of your buttock would go numb. Then after you did readjust, that once numb part of the buttock would tingle for several long, uncomfortable minutes. And then there was the cold to tend with.

Ron found the house and steered the van up a long, winding driveway bordered by high weeds. The house rose up from the weeds reflecting enough moonlight to make out myriad odd angles against a dark sky. For some reason Ron nosed the van around and we opened the back door and watched breathlessly as he backed deeper into the front yard and closer to the house. I feared a rush of zombies. That we'd be screaming "Go! Go! Go!" and Ron would be busy studying the side mirrors, careful not to scrape the paint on a fence post, and never see the stream of undead filing into the back of the van and making dinner of us all. Finally, he stopped. I'd never heard things so quiet and still—as ghosts, *right?* Slowly we unfolded out of the van and into the cold air and the weedy yard. Some of us had flashlights and bounced the yellow ball over broken gutters and gaping holes where long before windows had been salvaged (stolen?). Ron led the way and as a group we crept, as close as we could possibly creep without stepping on one another, up to what looked like the front of the house. As we crept, Ron narrated for us just what had happened all those years before.

"And then the father—the husband—made his way along *this* very porch," he said, as he led us along loose and uneven boards. "To this window right here." He stopped in front of a window that gaped from floor to ceiling, larger than a door. And so we stepped through the same portal as the ax murderer had so long ago. Ron continued the narrative: "Once he . . . he. . . ." Ron searched for words, and we tried to help him by collectively leaning forward, our breath making fog in the sparse light. "Wendell," Ron said, "why don't you finish telling us the story?"

Wendell worked as a florist and immediately began to spin one fancy bouquet of a story. "So the husband creeps this way." Wendell took a couple of steps and we followed him. ". . . to where the bed was." He made a boxy gesture with his hands to indicate that he was now standing over the exact spot where the wife had laid, snoring soundly possibly. Wendell turned a light onto his face and said, "He paused over her bed and studied the sleeping figure, tortured with the deed he was contemplating. But the dye was cast. He gripped his axe and the weight of it seemed to multiply as he raised it high above his head." He raised the light and the yellow beam could have been a glint of steel. "High above his true love and the mother of his children and then—"

A sharp noise from outside halted Wendell's axe in mid-chop. I turned and, through the window, saw a bouncing yellow light, shredded by the weeds, but moving closer. I heard voices, mumblings. *Ghosts!* No one inside the house stirred. No one inside the house said a word. Wendell's imaginary axe was useless to us. But Ron's flashlight wasn't. He aimed it through the window, into the weeds and called out, "Who's there?"

The light in the weeds went black. The mumblings ceased. I heard a pounding, like a drum, then realized it was my heart and maybe the collective beating of the other ten. Still no one said a word. A cackle came out of the darkness. Then a male voice called out, "You scared us, man!" The yellow came back on and stabbed in through the window and bounced around the room. "Where you guys from?" said the voice. We breathed again and moved about in the dark and acted like the presence of the college kids from across town was a bother. Disappointed they weren't ghosts. Relieved they weren't ghosts.

Wendell's part of the show was over. There were only five visitors, but they were loud and giddy and poked around the house and made fake ghost sounds and cracked lame ax murderer jokes. So we loaded up in the van and left the haunted house. The temperature was still falling and the adrenaline was no longer flowing. Everyone got cold. Very, very cold.

The van's heater was capable but for only the two seats up front. Not the slightest wafting of warm air made its way to the back. More than buttocks were going numb. Jeff, Mike, Luke, Wendell, Tim and John, Jon, and Jonathan and I stood to freeze separately or, there was another way to stay warm. I'm not sure who suggested it. And at first there was some reluctance to getting so . . . *close*. But when the guy on the bottom would report back with news like "IT'S SO WARM!" then the closeness was no longer strange, but necessary. "It's so warm," rose up muffled and baked from deep inside. "Okay, time's up. My turn," would ring out in the cold and bounce around on the steel from someone on the outer layer. And the pile would shift, turn inside out, and a new guy had his two minutes in the oven. We lay on the van's chilly metal bottom, interlaced like basketweave. Wrapped up like a ball of yarn. Knotted together like knuckles in a clasp. Overlapping like pages in a tome. Bound like the seat of a lawn chair. Jeff, Mike, Luke, Wendell, Tim and John, Jon, Jonathan, and I—and eventually Jerry—swallowed our pride and shared our heat. The kind of heat that could only come from the living.

Yeah, I was alive then. Very much so.

As a zombie, my kids took me on a fishing trip for Father's Day. Since the river runs through our backyard, we didn't have to travel very far. At that time I didn't have a boat—but that was about to change.

Chera and her husband Craig made me wait inside while they scurried around and tried to keep everything a secret. Zach was down by the river, but I couldn't tell what he was doing. Chera and Craig packed a cooler with soft drinks, cookies, Nutty Buddy bars, pudding, and peanut butter and crackers—all my favorites.

When all seemed to be ready, they led me to the river with our hands filled with fishing poles and tackle boxes. "Surprise!" they called out when they couldn't keep the bright blue and yellow raft a secret any longer. Zach stood up straight with a couple of blue oars in his hands. "That's a lot of pumping," he said, shaking one arm as if to loosen the cramping of all that pumping the air that it'd taken to fill the little raft.

At first I thought they were going to get me settled in and then push me off. Then Chera revealed that we were *all* going. "At once?" I asked.

"It's a four-man raft," she said. "It says so on the box."

And there were four of us. Okay. So off we went. The part of the river behind our house is shallow, so we waded in and I hoisted one leg over the edge and stepped into the raft, sitting on the edge with one foot in and one foot out. The front end shot up and Craig caught it on its way up and rode it back into the water. He sat on the front to hold it down while and Chera and Zach came in from each side. I quickly discovered that sitting in the bottom wouldn't work. The raft was more like a waterbed and not a very firm one. When I tried that, two things happened. One, my rear end would be a couple of feet below the surface and I could barely see over the pillowy sides. And two, sitting in the bottom of the boat caused everyone else to slide to the middle. So we all sat on the edges with our feet resting in the bottom. We weaved the fishing poles in between the four of us, and Zach and Chera took hold of the oars and pushed us off into the river's deeper waters.

It took a couple of hundred yards before the paddlers got the hang of keeping the raft straight. If Chera took a longer stroke than Zach (or vice versa) the front end would swing wide and we'd change directions, always moving from one side of the river to the other. Once we got going though, Craig and I decided to fish. My first cast over my children's heads went high into a tree. I tried to yank it loose but instead pulled us under some low-hanging, snaky-looking limbs. Chera swatted with her oar at anything that moved. Zach poked at things with his, whether it moved or not. Craig told us all that he loved us in case he died in the next few minutes. We were there only a few minutes. Once we were free, we zigzagged on downstream, oars and rods clanking together like battle weapons. I caught a small bass and the fish spun us in circles.

We made it to a wide rocky area where we beached the raft and fished from the bank and soaked up the sun and ate all our junk food. After a couple of hours we paddled back, zigzagging upstream. We passed a boat occupied by a man and a woman going in the other direction. One sat at each end of the boat, in a nice, comfortable-looking seat—with cushions and back rests. They made their casts without any interference. When one of them moved in the least, the other did not bounce or have to steady himself to keep from falling off the edge and into the water. A whisper-quiet motor propelled them in a straight line. We waved as our ships passed there on the narrow river. Then I cast my lure into a tree and together, in our four-man raft, we went after it. Swinging, poking, praying, and laughing. The two people in the giant boat motored off, whisper quiet. And though together, at opposite ends of their big boat, they appeared to be rather lonely.

~

Though we seemed dead, we did but sleep.

—Shakespeare—of all people

~

9

Tower of Terror and Other Near-death Experiences

Back when I was alive, the kids took me to ride the Tower of Terror. Chera was sixteen and Zach was eleven. I was fine to stroll around MGM grounds there in Orlando, eat popcorn, and have the kids pose with characters like Spider Man and the Power Rangers. But the kids shamed me into climbing on board and taking a quick ride with death.

We climbed into one big car with about six other people and began our ride on the ground floor of what appeared to be a six-story building by riding to the top in an oversized elevator. At the top the door opened and everything looked like a hotel, the long hallway, the guest room doors with numbers on them. Only there was scary music playing and people screaming in the distance and from behind the closed doors. The lights were dim—spooky. Our car rolled out of the elevator and I was expecting a short tour of the place. Maybe some of the doors would open and we'd see body parts and masked people with chainsaws. Maybe air would blow in our faces and we'd all scream. I was looking forward to the scary tour. That's when the bottom fell out.

Just like that we were falling! I hate the sensation of falling, absolutely hate it! Everything blacked out. A bright light flashed. Then, contrary to all laws of physics, we weren't falling anymore, but going up. Then we fell again. Up and down, up and down. My insides were confused. Finally the car stopped and we rolled out into daylight. Inside people were screaming. Outside, people were laughing. I laughed and told the kids how cool that was. They thought so. Before we exited the gate, there was a booth where you could see a picture of yourself riding the Tower of Terror. The kids bellied up to the counter and scanned the photos hanging there. Zach spotted it first. He seemed excited, and then his face went slack. He frowned. He turned to me and said, "Dad? Were you scared?"

When I saw the picture I could see why he thought so. Chera and Zach had their hands raised high, their heads tilted back, eyes wide open, and mouths open in a full laugh-scream. Me? I was curled up in the corner of the car, eyes squinted shut, teeth clenched, squeezing the safety bar. I could have been praying.

"Whoa, Dad," was all Chera could say.

We walked out into the crowded park but I felt very much alone. I couldn't live like this. "Come on, kids," I said, making a U-turn and heading back to the Tower of Terror. "We're going to do this again."

Back up the tower we went. Down the same spooky hallway. Only this time I was ready for it. When the bottom fell out, I threw my arms up over my head. I screamed and laughed. And since I wasn't sure when the camera would flash, I did that the whole time—more than anyone else in our car. I'm sure everyone believed I was having one fun time.

When the car finally came to a stop, I led the way to the picture booth and found our shot right away. "Look at that, kids! Look at your dad!"

"All right! Way to go, Dad!"

We walked into the park and I bought ice cream for the three of us.

Yeah, I was alive then. Very much so.

As a zombie I had some business to do in Toronto and I asked Zachary to come along with me. I think the main reason he said yes was because he had a baggie filled with Canadian coins. Over the years we'd collected more than a handful of these coins that are useless here in the states. Vending machines spit them out. The currency exchange won't take them. The banks won't take them. "They only take paper money," Zach lamented. He knew this because he tried every bank in town. There's about $25 worth of coins in the bag and Zach burned up two tanks of gas to find out this information. So maybe he went because of the coins. And also because of the roller coasters. I bribed him with Canada's tallest roller coaster—Behemoth. I hate roller coasters, but I wanted Zach to be there with me. He agreed. He drug his suitcase out and the first thing he dropped in was that baggie filled with Canadian coins.

Business was over and we were driving just north of Toronto to Canada's Wonderland. Zach had slipped on some headphones and was playing air drums with reckless abandon when I pointed through the front window. At the sight of the bright yellow arches—that had nothing to do with hamburgers—that rose above the trees and buildings just a short distance from the highway, Zach raked a hand through his hair and stopped the music momentarily. Just then seats filled with people strapped in them reached the top of the largest arch and then disappeared in a flash, arms flailing in the direction of heaven, their silence eerie. "That's Behemoth," Zach said, the tone of his voice weighted with a certain amount of something like reverence. I chose not to speak for fear I might blubber in front of him.

On the way in the gate Zach had a little too much spring in his step and I had none. "Okay," I told him, "let's start with something slow and small. Sort of build our way up to it." *It* being Behemoth.

"Come on, Dad. You're not scared, are you?"

"I just like to pace myself." It was no secret to him that I hated roller coasters. Mostly I hated that sensation of falling. My worst nightmare (a reoccurring one at that) is one where I run past the edge of something high and can't stop and tumble off into nothing—just fall and fall and fall. But I'm sure that's normal—right?

There were metal detectors at the front gate and Zach set off the alarm. "You got any metal in your pockets?" the security officer asked him. Zach unsnapped a pocket on his cargo shorts and fished out the plastic bag filled with coins. The officer waved him on through, the sight of so much Canadian coin not the least bit odd to him.

I grabbed up one of the park maps, a cartoonish rendering of all the attractions, and spread it out on top of one of the park's trash cans. The map was extremely colorful and filled with squiggly lines: these were the roller coasters—fifteen in all. Zach was anxious to get started. Still studying the map, I found a coaster not far from the entrance, one that didn't appear to be too big. (Unlike Behemoth that jumped off the page and continued into the margins. It wouldn't have surprised me to see it continued on the other side.) The one we steered for was called Flight Deck. On the map it was just a smidge larger than the carrousel with plastic horses and all silver—a safe, muted color. This, I thought, would be a good place to start, not with the fiery reds and oranges and yellows of the others all splayed out on the map.

But on our way to Flight Deck we passed by something called Xtreme Flyer. Zach stopped. The jingle in his pocket went silent. His gaze turned upward. We stood beneath a giant arch, one that reminded me of that famous one in St. Louis. (I read later that this arch we stood beneath now is 170 feet high!) Just then three girls, strapped face-down into what looked like some sort of canvas gurney, dangled from a single cable that had been fastened to a network of harnesses all knotted together just above their backs. Another smaller cable, hooked to the same knot of harnesses, looped back and ended at the top of the arch. Then the smaller cable went taut and the girls began to rise—backward and toward the top of the arch. With arms locked together, they screamed and giggled and professed how much they didn't want to die.

Zach and I stood frozen there on the ground. We were right in their path. If the cable were to snap, we'd be bowled over. As the girls in the gurney rose, their screams and giggles fell from the sky like rain. I was feeling ill for them.

Then a voice on a PA system blared out, "Okay, enjoy your flight on three . . . two . . . one!"

One of the girls pulled a cord and the three of them fell and fell and fell. Hair flew back like swish marks. Screams were stifled momentarily. Six feet from the ground this ship of falling girls began to turn upward. The big cable pulled taunt and sent them into a smooth arc that sliced the air above us. We could hear their clothes and hair and skin creating friction against the invisible air, making the sound of a match against a strike pad. The laughter and screams returned. Only now they seemed to have a tinge of relief. The expectant horror was replaced with exhilaration.

As the girls swung like a pendulum above our heads, Zach hitched a thumb in the direction of the arch and said, "We're doing this." As matter of fact as that. No discussion. Then he watched my eyes, to see if I'd waver. I knew what he was doing. He was on alert to sense the slightest hesitation. The shortest pause would drop me below "screaming girls" in his estimation.

"All right," I said, making up for my poor acting skills by making a sudden move to the line where people waited in the sun just so they could fall, fall, fall.

The harness they wrapped around us was more like a big padded apron. I stepped into it while this kid connected, looped, and snapped things behind me where I couldn't see. He asked me to pick up this trapeze-like bar and carry it over to the staging area with Zach. I was a bit concerned because everything seemed to fit way too loose. Above us two grown men screamed like babies, their bodies making a whooshing sound through the air. As we waited for our turn, sweating in our padded aprons, the song blaring out of the park speakers seemed to mock me: *it's the end of the world as we know it, and I feel fine.* Later, a young married couple flew by. As their swinging slowed, I heard her complain to him that he'd pulled the cord on one. That she'd expected an extra beat after the one. Really? You almost died and you're complaining about a half second?

We were next when the phone rang—the one on the other side of the gate where the small child (seemed to me anyway) led people to and from the giant cable. At first she ignored the ringing. She helped a group get unharnessed. Then she answered the phone after the zillionth ring. "Yeah, okay, okay, now? Yeah, I'll try." She hung up. She approached Zach and me and I was sure she was going to tell us about the fray in the cable that the kid in the souvenir shop had spotted while on break. "Just turn around and let me check your harnesses real quick."

"Take all the time you need," I told her. "Don't want to miss anything back there." She tugged and lifted and shook things back there and seemed real pleased with how the other child had lashed us in. "Is it supposed to be this loose?" I asked, but she was already opening the gate and leading us through.

We stepped up onto a platform where the married couple was just catching their breath. "How was it?" I asked.

The man shook his head and issued a single word: "intense."

Behind us another child joined the first and they proceeded to clip and hook things together. One would lift something and someone else would pull something over and a carabineer would click, and they did this with such speed that I wanted to whistle really loud and bring it all to a halt and ask them, "Can we just go over all the connections one more time, only this time nice and *slow*?"

"All right," one child in sunglasses said, "who's pulling the rip cord?" I'd given that task to Zach. I was afraid I would freeze. "Lock arms together so you don't smack each other on the way down. I'll count down three, two, one and you can pull the cord. Have a nice flight." He patted the knot of cords and carabineers that mere children had orchestrated back there, out of my view and impossible to inspect, and we began to move—backwards and up.

Zach kept saying, "Oh, man. Oh, man. Higher. Higher."

I couldn't say a word. I did breathe a lot though. I figured if these were my last ones, I'd pack'em in here at the end. As we rose and people got smaller and we could see beyond the park and into the parking lot, suddenly the yellow peaks of Behemoth seemed like a kiddie ride. Oh, how I ached for the simple Behemoth! The cable came to a halt with a jar. We should think about this, I thought. Then the voice from the ground rose up: "Alright, all clear and ready for flight!" *No!* "On three . . . two . . . one." Give me one more beat. *One more precious half second!* This was just like my nightmare. From the side I could see Zach's hand going for the rip cord. Then just like that we were falling, falling, falling. . . .

The apron was oh-so-snug now as we raced to the ground at eighty miles an hour. But incredibly, the fear seemed to have been ripped away, if by nothing else than the sheer speed. The reoccurring nightmare I have—skidding over the edge and tumbling into nothing—was so much worse than this. This fall, from Xtreme Flyer, was actually full of life.

Trees, people, and green, green grass seemed to rush up to me as I rushed down to them. Air smashed into my face and into my lungs, threaded its way through my hair and over my scalp. Tears painted my temples and rushed into my ears. A scream worked its way up from somewhere deep inside, one, I realized almost immediately, that echoed that of my son, who fell into life, locked arm-in-arm right beside me.

After that we rode Jet Scream, Vortex, Thunder Run, Mine Buster, Dragon Fire, Wild Beast (this one right after lunch, no problems), Time Warp, Flight Deck, Sky Rider, and, yes, Behemoth. We rode them all with eyes wide open and hands held high, the same posture you'd take when trying to grab hold of all the life you can. What we learned is that the wooden roller coasters will give you kidney damage, and if you climb into a car that has padded headrests, you're probably about to get your ears boxed.

At the end of the day Zach still jingled with coins. "How about a nice ice cream cone?" he asked me. So we found a little shop and placed our order. Zach fished out the bag of Canadian coins and took great pleasure in counting out $7. We ate the ice cream on the way to the parking lot, trying to finish them before the sun could claim them. "This is the only thing I bought all day," he said, waggling the chocolate bar before him. "Kept waiting for that *perfect* thing to buy, you know."

"Save it," I told him, "for the next time we come to Canada." Then I returned to my ice cream cone, one that was absolutely perfect.

⁓

Suddenly there's no more mystery
Feels like you're the other half of me
We've only just begun
But look what love has done
Our two hearts beat as one.

—H & Claire, pop duo

⁓

What Really Killed King Kong

10

Back when I was alive, I was on the high school wrestling team.
Coach massaged each arm by rolling my bicep between his palms, as if
my arm was a stick and he was trying to start a fire.

"Okay, Poothead," he said. He called everyone Poothead, not just
me. I'd weighed in at 126 pounds. Coach was my height, probably 150
pounds at most, with short-cropped blond hair and a pooched-out
bottom lip because of the tobacco he harbored there. "You just go out
there and give it the best you can." I was pretty sure I detected a tone of
acquiescence. "You've come a long ways and can be proud." I looked at
Coach, but that was the best he was going to give me. He wasn't looking
at me, but at my opponent across the mat. This was the regional level
and the winner would go to the state tournament. No one from our
high school had ever gone to the state tournament before. Technically,
he weighed the same as me: 126 pounds. But he must have had hollow
bones or ate helium for breakfast or was made of balsa wood. His biceps

99

were swollen, his chest puffed up. Even his ears had muscles. Even his muscles had muscles. I was no wimp, but I guess from Coach's perspective, I was outgunned here.

Tournament days were usually long days with big breaks between rounds. I had won an earlier match and then Coach took several of us to see a movie. It was a remake of *King Kong* with Jessica Lange. King Kong didn't have perfect takedowns, or reversals, or cross-body rides, or half-nelsons. But he could throw down, and he always wound up on top. It wasn't always about style with King Kong. It was about results. And that was inspiring—even if Coach wasn't at that moment. He released my arm to retrieve a cup that he spit some dark ooze into and told me good luck once more—just before I would face off with King Kong.

I stepped onto the mat, onto that familiar spongy feel under my feet. I adjusted my head gear, just to keep my hands busy before the perfunctory handshake. The referee gave his spiel about rules and safety issues, squared us off, and then blasted his whistle. In an instant King Kong flew at me from across the circle. I braced myself.

At the edge of the mat, on either side of Coach and his cup, knelt my teammates, my vociferous teammates. Three of us had made it to the regionals. Six others had come along to cheer us on. Their voices slipped around the foam padding of my headgear. Their collective voices prompted me to layout flat when I saw the blur of muscles move toward my legs—the proper defensive move. Their voices gave me the wherewithal to hook my arms under each of his armpits and the strength to turn Kong over onto his back—all before Coach could work up a good spit.

At the edge of the mat cheered Sylvester Kelley. Sly was no more than five feet tall and weighed 98 pounds—post cheeseburger. He was all muscle and slippery as a trout. At practice he'd actually slip through cradles and leg locks as if he were a thread passing through a needle's eye. Now he pounded the mat's edge and yelled my name (Pierce, not Poothead) and when I did something right, like turn over King Kong and score two points, I heard him laugh. I wanted to stop and give him a hug, but I had both arms filled with someone who wanted to crush me, and there were at least three minutes to go in the match.

Next to Sly was Bill Ledbetter. He was 119 pounds and came to our school his sophomore year from Colorado with a reputation and his own mythology. We didn't know how they wrestled in Colorado or what kind of super strength the mountain air might have given him. Since we were close in weight class, he was my practice partner. There's no way to know who was more competitive. When we ran laps, we raced. When Coach tried to break us down, he couldn't break either of us. When we practiced, we tried to hurt each other in semi-legal ways, like adding extra pressure with an elbow, or digging into a breastbone with a bony chin, or squeezing a cradle harder than necessary. As far as I remember neither of us complained, no one whined. There were grunts and frustrated sounds like "Arrggh!" More than anything, we each pushed back and squeezed and dug a little harder. We grew tough together.

Sometimes (many times) we'd find ourselves a pound or two over on the day of a match. I've lost five pounds in a day before. So has Bill. Many times we did it together. If we turned on all the shower heads in the locker room to full hot, it'd create a cloud of steam so thick you couldn't see from one side to the other. And if I wore two sweat pants and three sweat shirts and did jumping jacks for an hour, I'd sweat off at least three pounds. Sometimes I'd spot Bill through the cloud of steam, only partially, looking more like a bird flapping futilely for lift off. If I still needed to lose another pound, I'd get a Coke bottle and a piece of gum. The gum helped me work up a spit. I'd carry the bottle with me everywhere I went until weigh-in, slowly filling it up. More than once Bill and I would cross paths in the hallway. Each with his own Coke bottle filled with a bubble gum-pink liquid. I never held Bill's bottle. But mine was always warm, at least body temperature.

From close by I could hear Bill's voice, thin and tinny, cheering me on, but mostly calling out moves and counter-moves. He was always the strategist. With fifteen seconds to go I led by one, but Kong was on the move. He'd nearly slipped away. An escape would tie things up and send this match into overtime. I hung on to his lower leg, squeezed harder than I ever had Ledbetter or tried to squeeze Sly. Dug my chin into his soft calf.

I heard Ledbetter and Sly exhorting me to hang on. And so did Steve and Wendell, Freddie and Todd, Barry and Butch. "Hang on!" they collectively chanted. Even Coach's tobacco-muffled "Hang on!" gave me strength to squeeze harder. At the sound of the whistle I went slack. The leg slipped away, but it meant nothing. The match was over. I pictured King Kong toppling from the top of the Empire State Building.

The referee made the win official by raising my hand. Then my teammates surrounded me and whacked me on the back, slapped me on the rear, and patted me on the head, and every strike I accepted as a gift. Even Coach's "Way to go, Poothead!" caused me to throw my arms around his neck. Across the mat I saw my opponent walk off, head down, fumbling with the strap of his headgear. His coach glared at me. I wanted to tell him it wasn't all me who killed the beast, but Sly, Bill, Steve and Wendell, Freddie and Todd, Barry and Butch. We did it together.

Yeah, I was alive then. Very much so.

As a zombie, the first time I ever went to "rehab," I went because of love. My wife was there, in a very expensive place in Scottsdale, Arizona, working out her issues. She was depressed. We'd done all the preliminary work in Nashville and her counselor told her about this place in Arizona, in fact had recommended it. But they didn't want me to go—not until week two, they'd said. So I sat at home wondering and worrying about what was going on. Chonda is not good alone. She doesn't do solitary very well. At the beginning of week two, I flew out and took a shuttle from the airport to the hotel. Chonda was in surprisingly good spirits when I met up with her. How could that be?

She had a rental car and knew the route from the hotel to the counseling center, so she drove. It was 8 A.M. and she and I were sitting in a circle of at least fifteen people. The director of this morning's group was older than me, gray-haired and had an air of authority. Dr. Earl, they called him. He asked us to check in. I didn't know what that meant. Luckily, I wasn't the first to go. The man to the left of Dr. Earl talked about his predilection for alcohol, how hard it was to come in this morning, but that he was glad he had—being here made him want to drink less. The next person had a problem with pornography. The next person was depressed and hadn't thought about killing himself in the last twenty-four hours. My wife admitted she was depressed and was looking for answers. Then Dr. Earl asked me to "check in." I was there because Chonda was there. I was sure there was a mistake and that I wasn't supposed to be talking, only listening. But that air of authority nudged me on. "I'm here," I began, "because my wife is depressed. I want to help her. I want her back. So I want to do whatever it takes to help my wife. I want to be the best husband I can be." I think I even used hand gestures that exuded determination.

Dr. Earl smiled, making me think I'd just delivered the best possible answer—maybe ever in the history of this counseling center. I'd nailed it! I was a psychological genius and I didn't even have a degree.

"Okay," Dr. Earl proclaimed. "I'll see you all in about three hours."

For the next three hours I visited with three different licensed psychologists. I talked about my parents, my childhood, my wife, God, my alcoholic father, my trauma egg, my circle of influence, and cried three separate times. When we assembled for group the next time, I heard similar stories of addictions and "acting out" and fears and failures. When it came to be my turn I told Dr. Earl, "I know that earlier I said I came here to help my wife. But what I want to say now is that *I'm messed up!*" I even pounded my chest King Kong-like so that there'd be no confusion about who I was talking about. I wanted to know more about *me*. I wanted answers about what had happened to me along the way. What had broken and how? And could I be put back together again? But I only had four days and that just didn't seem to be enough time. The issue of codependency alone could keep any counselor and me busy for weeks.

I didn't even know what codependency was before that week. Dr. Earl asked us to check in and say something about our codependency issues. I was first. So I asked for a good definition. Dr. Earl smiled and said, "Let's go around the room and I'm sure you'll catch on." By the time it got back to me I raised my hand and said, "Oh yeah, I'm real codependent. On the way out here I sat by the window on the airplane. About an hour before we landed, I had to go to the bathroom. But I didn't want to be a bother to the two women between the aisle and me. So I held it. And it was painful. But I couldn't ask them to please let me pass. I think that's codependent." Dr. Earl smiled at me and nodded and said, "Oh yeah. Very." I was so very pleased to learn they had a name for the way I felt.

Two years passed before I decided to do an intensive counseling session of my own. Me being a Zombie had a lot to do with that. I contacted a place in town and told them what I was looking for. The director of counseling designed a program targeted for me and my "codependent tendencies" (that's what she called it). But that's not all. The program also was designed to deal with issues like anger, hurt, worry, boundaries, and anything else I happened to mention during a brief intake interview, like a sense of abandonment that had hung like a pall over me for so long—making me feel dead. It was a five-day program. I started at 9 A.M. on a Monday and went until 6 P.M. that first night.

I talked about my marriage a lot that week. About the times I had hurt and the times I had hurt her. We talked about love languages and forgiveness. I watched videos that were supposed to help me understand myself and my wife. I talked about moving out and getting an apartment. I even drove by a neat apartment unit with a "For Rent" sign in the yard. I could start over, I told my counselor. Concern crinkled his brow. My counselor, trained and licensed, said, "Hmmmm." Then he grabbed a Bible from his desk. He opened it somewhere near the middle and began flipping pages. "In Genesis 2:24 WEB it says, 'Therefore a man will leave his father and his mother, and will join with his wife, and they will be one flesh.' In Ephesians 5:31 WEB it says, 'For this cause a man will leave his father and mother, and will be joined to his wife. The two will become one flesh.' In Mark 10 Jesus refers to Genesis when he says, '. . . and the two will become one flesh. So they are no longer two, but one.'" He looked up from the book to me, brow still crinkled. "What do you suppose that means?"

After all those years removed from school, I still have that undergraduate mentality. I always want to get the answers right. "Obviously we could never physically be one flesh," I said, then paused to check his expression for a clue that I was on the right track. "So I think it means we'd be one spirit (?)"

"Exactly."

Yes!

"God has made you and Chonda one flesh. The world tries to come between you. So let's see how we can get back there. But it won't be easy. And it can wear you out."

I wished they had a video that would help me with that.

I also talked *ad nauseam* that week about my father. He was an alcoholic and died when I was twenty-three, just two months before Chonda and I were married. No matter who I talked to about dad that week, every counselor would eventually ask, "So was your father also abusive?"

"No," I would say. "When he got drunk, he would sit in his chair and tell me how much he loved me." He'd be practicing the worst thing—drinking—but telling me the best thing in the world: that he loved me. Sometimes he would even reach out a hand and shake mine, like we were meeting for the first time, and say, "I want you to know how much I love you." And he wouldn't stop shaking it until I responded. Sometimes he'd take my hand in both of his and try to pull me closer, making me look into his rheumy eyes. Later, I would tell the counselors how I always rejected that love because I couldn't believe it. If he really loved me he wouldn't hurt me by drinking like he was. The power of love could make him stop, couldn't it?

After four days of intensive counseling, I'd picked up a few more definitions, a few more word pictures of what codependency looks like, a few more exercises to help me create a habit of being assertive and less passive. Lots of blanks on worksheets to fill out sometime later, after I'd given things more thought. But more than anything I seemed to have stirred this big old pot filled with everything from my insides, so that everything was now a big soupy mess. No more layers, at least. Now everything touched everything else. I just wasn't sure how yet. That answer would come Friday morning in a way I could never have expected or imagined.

Friday morning I almost didn't show up. I knew what was on the schedule and I didn't want to do it. Back on Monday when I'd heard my schedule for Friday I'd made up my mind then that I would play hooky. I'd heard about this exercise, this Theophostic Prayer, before. "We'll go back to a time in your life that was painful," Robert told me (he would be the one walking me through this). "We're going to take that scene, that memory, and we're going to bring Jesus into that scene." It all sounded a little weird to me.

And it just kept getting weirder when Robert said, "Go back to a time when you felt abandoned. Play it like a video. And let me see it."

I took a deep breath. I thought of the moment right away. "It's when Dad and I moved out. We left Mom. I was fifteen. Dad had just had surgery. Had over half of his stomach removed and it hadn't gone well because infection had set in and he couldn't get around at all. I figured I'd better take care of him. So we moved out. Dad found a small house trailer. It was winter time so it was cold. It was dark and musty. We bought some pots and pans at a salvage store and a black-and-white TV."

I paused and Robert jumped in: "Now invite Jesus into that trailer."

Oh, how I ached to have to do this! I was embarrassed. But just like that I saw Jesus standing there. The kind of Jesus you see on posters: full beard, long hair, and wearing a robe with big sleeves. Dad was in the only chair we owned, leaning forward toward the TV. We had a sofa that I was sure was made of plastic. The edges were cracked and the cracks pinched the backs of my knees if I happened to be wearing shorts when I sat on it. I asked Jesus to have a seat. He did, on the plastic sofa.

"And what would you say to him?"

I thought about this and ordered my words. "Please make Dad stop drinking. Touch him. Wave a hand over him. Blow your breath on him. Just make him stop."

"And what would Jesus say?"

The words came, but I didn't like them. "He'd say, 'I know you hurt, but I'm here with you. I have something for you to do one day. And this is a part of it. Trust me.'" Then in my "vision" Jesus repeated himself: "Please trust me on this."

Robert said, "Tell Jesus what you worry about."

I dabbed my eyes because the tears had started and wouldn't stop. "I worry about Dad. I worry about his health. I worry about leaving him alone. I worry about what I might find when I come home. I worry that I might not be able to trust you."

"Now picture what that worry looks like," Robert said. "Personify it."

I didn't have to think too long about it. I saw that worry. It was a large tumor that filled both my hands. The color of a bruise—smelly, viscous, and sticky.

"Now give it to Jesus."

I handed it off to my guest and he took it freely. A slimy film stuck to his hands, but he didn't seem to mind.

"What's he doing?" Robert asked.

"He's taking it," I said. "And he's putting it somewhere. I can't see where, but he's getting rid of it."

We did the same thing with anger. "What's it look like?"

"It's a stick, a club," I said. "Only there are thorns covering the whole thing. It hurts my hands to hold it."

"Now give it to Jesus."

"But . . ." I did. Jesus took it. The thorns stuck his hands and there was blood. He grimaced and took the thorny-clubbed anger and put it somewhere I couldn't see.

Then Robert wanted me to talk to Jesus about loneliness. "Tell him how you've felt lonely."

"Jesus, I feel like I've been so lonely for so long. Mom disappeared. My dad was always drinking, always gone in his mind. And you, God. Where were you? I kept asking for your help and you were nowhere to be found. Why? And now I have a fear that I may be alone again."

"Tell him how much you hurt," Robert said.

I wanted to point to the half-box of Kleenex I'd used. I thought it was pretty clear how much I hurt. But I told him anyway. I couldn't

see the hurt. There was no shape or characteristics like there had been
when I personified worry and anger. But I knew it was heavy. "Give it
to Jesus." I held out my heavy hand and Jesus reached out too. He took
the hurt that I couldn't see, but certainly felt the weight of. Only this
time Jesus touched me, on the hand. Then he took my hand and began
to shake it, as if we were meeting for the first time. "I love you," Jesus
said. "Then he wrapped both his hands around mine and continued to
shake my hand, saying over and over, "I love you. I love you. I love you."

Then suddenly it wasn't Jesus anymore, but my father in his chair.
Me standing over him, he leaning toward me and looking up. "I love you,"
came his familiar statement. "I love you." His eyes rimmed with tears.

Robert stopped talking and let me live with that moment. All the
times I'd felt alone and abandoned, God had been there all along—his
love pushing out through my father. His love falling all over me in those
simple words and in that simple handshake.

The worry and anger were now tucked away in a Jesus lockbox.
The hurt had been comforted. The sense of abandonment revealed as
a lie. I was not alone and had never been. And no matter what would
happen in my life now, I would never be alone again. As Robert had
promised, in those weird beginning moments, Jesus had slipped into
those memories and changed everything.

Robert wanted me to describe the trailer we lived in once more—the
unredeemed trailer, he called it. "It's small and cramped. And dark. So
dark. There's no color anywhere. Even the TV is black-and-white. And
it's cold. A blanket of cold covers us, but rather than keep us warm, it
seems to draw warmth from us. This is where I live."

"Now what would that redeemed trailer look like—now that Jesus
is there?"

I hadn't thought of redeeming the trailer before. See how weird
this got?

109

"Windows everywhere!" I said before I could think too much. "All around the tiny trailer a long row of windows circle. Windows where there shouldn't even be windows. Light crisscrosses the trailer, dissects the air and space into bright, yellow pieces. Like a kaleidoscope. Jesus even kicks open the door—one of those tip-over-the-money-changer kicks—to let even more light into the room. And there we are: Me, Dad, and Jesus bathed in a warm, heavenly light. In truth." Robert allowed me time to update that memory file and then tuck it away, into a place I can find it easily and with instructions to review it often. He allowed me to wipe my eyes and blow my nose. Then we stood and he gave me a big hug and thanked me. For what?

"For allowing me to see Jesus again." So I had to thank him for allowing me to see him for the first time.

Later, when I told Chonda what had happened, what I had seen, she wrapped her arms around me and we pressed so close together that I could feel her heart beating against my chest. We stood there, in the living room of our home, clinging to one another, breathing in and out as one flesh.

~

*You'll know it's your purpose when it [your work]
accomplishes two things: one, it's fulfilling and, two, it's
fruitful—and when you do it you come alive.*

—Rick Warren, *Meet the Press*, November 29, 2009

~

*This motor's caught its wind and brought me back to life.
Now I'm alive and well.*

—"Alive and Well," Kenny Chesney and Dave Matthews

~

11

One Man's Garbage Is Another Man's Lesson Plan

Back when I was alive, I worked as a garbage man the summer I turned sixteen. I'd ride on the back of the truck as it careened through neighborhoods, making wide turns that forced me to hang on tight with one hand while leaning far out, my free arm outstretched for balance, like one of those rodeo people who ride a barebacked bull while standing up. And because I was sixteen, I would wave at girls who drove by or who stood on the corner, believing they were wishing I weren't moving so fast so they could talk to me, maybe get my phone number. But I was only sixteen.

We worked in pairs on giant trucks that held tons of household garbage. I worked with a man named Roger. He was a hippy. The first hippy I'd ever known. He wore a scruffy, untrimmed beard and had long, straight, shoulder-length hair. (In the mid-70s, anyone with long hair was considered a hippy.)

We worked in the most affluent part of Nashville called Belle Meade. (This is where Al Gore bought his mansion once he settled back home.) The people of Belle Meade threw away stuff that was way better than what Roger and I owned. That's why we both—maybe even every garbage man—had his own basket wired up somewhere on the truck. You find something you like, toss it in your basket, and take it home.

These houses usually sat far off the main road and there was no way to drive the truck back to where the can was, and there was no way the people of this neighborhood would wheel their cans to the curb. Besides, many of the cans were underground for aesthetic reasons. A simple foot pedal would open the lid and a strongman (me) would lift them out.

It was Roger who taught me how to be a garbage man. He demonstrated how you take the big plastic drum from off the truck, hoist it onto your shoulder, and hike it to the back of the house, where the garbage can usually was. Then we'd empty the contents of the customer's can into the plastic one we carried—as much as we could carry. Then you'd hoist it onto your shoulder and carry it back to the truck. Going in was easy, coming out. . . .

Sometimes it'd take me two or three trips to service one house. If it rained the night before, the garbage was usually waterlogged. If there was a celebration the night before (like the celebration of Saturday and Sunday), the cans were often loaded with liquor bottles—glass is heavy.

Roger had a trick for lifting the heavy barrel. "First, get your knee under it, like this," he told me, swinging the barrel up just enough to get his right knee under the barrel's bottom. "Then . . ." and here he stopped talking and just demonstrated how to lower his knee, swivel the lower body, then clear the hips, and drive the right knee the plane of an arc that would send the knee up like an exaggerated march step and the barrel straight up into the air. Then all you had to do was step underneath the barrel before it started back down and let its bottom edge settle into that niche between your shoulder blade and earlobe, all the while hanging on to its handle with one hand and supporting the outer bottom edge with the other. Easy.

Roger made this look easy anyway. He was tall and wiry but could still send the heaviest of barrels into the sky and make it land in its comfortable niche there on the shoulder blade, like a lock and key. The whole routine took me a few tries—a few weeks—to master. Even then I'd still often wobble around in circles, trying to find my balance. Sometimes when I couldn't get the height of the lift just right, or my timing was off and I'd sense grave danger, I'd step out of the way and let the barrel plop back to the pavement. Sometimes I'd have to remove some of the garbage to lighten the load. And then there was always the juice to consider. Most of our plastic barrels had worn a hole somewhere along the bottom, and that soured juice would find its way out and trickle down our shoulders and arms and disappear beneath our waistbands. It took me a while to identify that smell, one I think that comes pretty close to soured corn.

Over all, the garbage business was great. We never slowed down. We never finished. Empty all the cans on a Monday and they were full again on Friday. If we'd been paid by the pound, we would have been millionaires. We should have at least received some sort of hazard pay since we were almost killed—twice. Once by an angry German Shepard, the other by a naked lady.

With our empty barrels on our shoulders, Roger and I entered a walled compound to collect the weekly refuse. We divided the load, shouldered our barrels, and headed out when Rover came after us—after Roger mainly. For some reason Roger set the dog off. Roger glanced back and then turned his back on the dog, who'd stopped and seemed to fall back on its haunches while extending its front legs and appeared ready to launch. Roger walked away. "Try not to pay any attention to him," he called to me over his empty shoulder and above the barking dog. He was teaching me how to survive. So I studied him as he walked away unnerved, oblivious of the beast. That's when Rover sprung forward and took a bite out of the back of Roger's upper thigh. Roger high-stepped it to pull loose and then, amazingly, kept hobbling forward, not looking back, not showing fear. The dog kept barking and stayed close. I followed along, sure I was doing a terrible job at hiding my fear, but I kept my barrel poised on my shoulder—like a weapon. I was probably showing panic, too. On my face I tried to convey the message: "If you come after me, I will pound you with this garbage!" I couldn't even imagine what that would look like, but I think Rover caught on because he stayed away and slinked on back to his mansion.

Roger hobbled the rest of the way to the truck and dumped the contents of his barrel before dropping his pants there on the side of the road to reveal, just below the hem of his boxers, at least two nasty-looking puncture wounds, connected in dot-to-dot fashion by smaller marks that would no doubt match the curve of the dog's incisors. A double stream of red trickled from the larger wounds down his pasty leg. Roger swore and then said, "I can't believe he bit me."

I didn't know what to say. I was wondering if maybe we needed a tourniquet. "Maybe he sensed your fear," I offered.

He pulled up his pants and we finished out the day, him hobbling and me wearing my don't-even-think-about-it scowl for any other canine we might encounter.

As the days passed and Roger didn't die or even foam at the mouth, we figured he'd be okay. He healed up and we kept collecting. Once again I was tacitly encouraged to "show no fear" when one morning we pushed through some boxwood hedges (if we loaded up a house and had room for more, we often took shortcuts through the hedges to the next house), and there stood a naked lady—*mostly* naked anyway. She had her back to us, naked from the waist down, using a garden hose to water some potted plants on her deck. Roger stopped and held out an arm, like you would do for a child who had not fastened his safety belt. We slowly lowered our barrels and made not a sound. I looked to Roger and he just shrugged. *Now* he showed fear. She must have sensed this. Because she glanced over her shoulder and spotted us—and screamed. She released the hose and dashed back inside, leaving a loop of city water shooting from the hose into the air behind her. Roger, hoisting his barrel onto his shoulder said, dryly, "Let's get the trash and get out of here!" While we loaded our barrels, water trickled off the deck like a Japanese water garden.

Thursdays always ended the same. At the end of our route was a small, far-from-ostentatious house, like the kinds we'd been working amid all day. At the side was a pair of metal cans in a wooden rack. On top, every Thursday, I could count on a cold soft-drink, a 7-UP, and a single quarter. Roger knew about it. Had known about it for the last two years he'd been working the route. Yet he always pulled back and let me take it alone. I never met the woman who lived there. Never even saw her. But the drink was always cold and wet with condensation. I'd always pocket the quarter and down the drink right then, hoping she was peeking from behind the curtains somewhere and witnessing how much this small act of kindness was appreciated.

I always looked forward to the ride home. One, the hard work was done. And two, I'd get to wave to the girl who always sat on the front porch of the yellow house. Oh yes, let me tell you about her. To get home we'd take a long, winding road through the country and along the river. Roger would drive and I would co-pilot, which meant I worked the radio. If a commercial came on, it was my job to find music—quickly. And then we'd sing, loud and uninhibited. Loud was necessary because we rode with the windows down to let the air race through the cab, bringing in its country freshness.

On one long stretch of green there stood a simple house not very far off the road at all. I could have emptied those garbage cans in a snap had it been on our route. But on the porch, every day, sat a girl in a chair. I never had more than a five-second glimpse because that's how long it took the garbage truck to race past. But five-seconds every day was enough to see she always wore shorts and a light-colored shirt—white or cream or yellow. And she had long, brown hair. Every day we'd pass and I would wave and Roger would blow the horn. Sometimes I'd lean out the window, and let the wind whip my T-shirt and wave long, deliberate waves. I liked to pretend I was arriving from a long journey, maybe from somewhere out on the sea and she was standing there and waving, her blouse all clean and white, her long brown hair lifting like a flag. Then our ship would roar past and I'd pretend that I was heading back out to sea and she was sending me off, wishing me a safe journey.

Once, after our ship sailed past, I looked back at Roger as he hugged the wheel, his hair whipping about his face, singing at the top of his lungs, and thought about how he allowed me a 7-UP and a quarter every Thursday, allowed me to sail in and sail out with a toot of the horn and a big armsy wave to the girl in the clean shirt, how he taught me about the garbage business, coached me to control my fear. Driving along the winding country road with fresh air washing over us, Roger even looked a little like Jesus.

But we both smelled of soured corn. Couldn't much help that.

Yeah, I was alive then. Very much so.

As a zombie, my colleague, Bob, called me into his office one day. "I'm going in tomorrow for some tests," he said as he ironed smooth the hand-written pages on his desk. "If anything should happen to me, here are the lesson plans for the next two days." The possibilities of what he meant by "should anything happen to me" hung in the air in the small office, only adding to the clutter of splayed English Literature textbooks and collections of hardbound critical analysis, student essays that had been abandoned, and one lamp—green with stringy fringe fencing in a low-wattage bulb.

I sort of swerved into being a professor. Hadn't planned on it at all and had not followed a curriculum for doing so. When I was thirty-five, I went back to graduate school and earned a Masters of Art in the field of English. I love that stuff—prose, poetry, drama. Basically I love to hear a good story. One day I gave a presentation on the history of the English language. This was a very ambitious task and I found ways to drag in words like quidnunc and sophistry. I used that old clichéd river metaphor, that whole "flowing" image is what I wanted. Not only was my presentation clichéd and trite, but it hardly scratched the surface of the true history of the English language. I told you it was an ambitious project.

Maybe I did okay, because afterwards my instructor suggested I sign on as a Teaching Assistant, which is really a misnomer. There is no *assisting*; it's all you, baby. In conjunction with this position, I took a "How to Teach" class. We wrote make believe theses, read old freshmen essays, and marked them up with red ink. Someone told me not to use red ink because it could hurt the students' self-esteem. So I went out and bought a giant pack of red pens because if me circling a pronoun-antecedent agreement problem was the worst thing that happened to them, I thought let's get it over with now so they can concentrate on bigger things—like finding a job! I made a note to myself to tell them how I used to be a garbage man and now I'm teaching them how to craft an essay.

On Monday I'd learn about "How to Discover a Thesis." On Tuesday I'd teach my class "How to Discover a Thesis." I felt more like a regurgitator than a teacher. We'd role play questions and answers. And if I didn't know the answer, I could always say, "I'll get back with you on that." After class I'd scramble to the library and dig through stacks of resources. I lived in fear of being found out.

Before my very first class as a college professor, I asked my professor who would introduce me.

"To whom?" she asked.

"To the class. Won't someone explain to them who I am? Where I'm from? Maybe list a few of my hobbies? Some theme music?"

"Oh no! Nothing like that. You walk in, slap your briefcase on the desk. Take off your glasses, swab them with a square of silky cloth. (Clearing your throat is another effective action.)"

I had twenty years on most of these students. I'd lived life hard, won, lost, suffered, celebrated, written, been published, and I knew what a thesis was, but I had never been so afraid.

I got to campus early for my eight o'clock class. I'll go to the student center, I told myself. I'll read a newspaper. The day before I'd gone to the classroom and gotten a feel for the room. I practiced scrawling my name on the chalkboard, waggled the neck of the overhead projector, flipped the light switch on and off again—using the edge of a textbook, like my arms were full and I was in a hurry to teach. I took pride in how I nonchalantly tossed a stub of chalk into the tray that ran along the bottom of the board and then knocked my hands together to rid them of dust. This was the most teacher-like thing I'd done so far. I believed I could replicate this, nervous or not.

Halfway through the thumbing of the pages of this newspaper, as I sat alone in the student center, I had a panicked thought: What if any of my students should walk through and later recognize me as the guy at the student center, the guy who was ridiculously early? *Is he nervous?* they would think, and I'd lose control—or at least respect. Quickly I stowed the paper and raced to the bathroom, and remained there for the next half hour.

At eight o'clock on the nose, I introduced myself to my first classroom. The title of "Professor Pierce" felt clumsy coming off my tongue. A professional emcee could have done much to pave the way for my entry. Maybe a fanfare? Some theme music? A brief bio that included something sad, certain to elicit a tear and garner some sympathy—like they do for those Olympic athletes we've never heard of, but suddenly we hear about a kidney transplant and now we're interested in the shot put more than any other sport? I explained who I was and what I expected. They fought against yawns. And I fought to keep from responding in kind.

One student named Phil didn't fully understand the syllabus, so he approached me at the end of the class and asked about it and I began to repeat myself, silently praying he didn't have questions I didn't know the answers to. Things were going just fine until the fire alarm sounded and we had to talk with raised voices. I was explaining to Phil why it would be a great idea to have his own textbook and not count on borrowing mine each day when a fireman stuck his head in the door and stabbed a finger in my direction and said, "You need to get out of here! Didn't you hear that alarm? This whole place could blow up!"

As an adult, as a leader, as a teacher, I told Phil, "We'd better get moving. Check the syllabus; the textbook information is on there." Then I herded him out of the building before it could blow up and ruin my first day.

About three weeks into the semester, just before Labor Day holiday, I met my colleague John in the parking lot. We were breaking for Labor Day. John looked tired. He always seemed to be in motion—a hand, a shoulder shrug, eyes blinking, head turning—twitchy. "Hey," he said, and I stopped and repositioned my too heavy bag on my shoulder. "You doing alright?"

I nodded. "Yeah. Looking forward to the time off."

He nodded back and then scanned the surroundings, as if he was concerned about being followed. "It will be nice." Then apropos of nothing, he said, "They ask an awful lot of questions, don't they?" He caught my gaze and then looked down.

In a strange way, his fear comforted me.

The semester passed and another one came. I tweaked my syllabus again and again and scoured the world for more resources. I approached each new semester with the eye of a teacher, which simply means—"I bet I could talk about *that* in class!"

I taught composition and argumentative writing and an introduction to literature. A Shakespearean play would remind me of a cartoon I once saw, so we'd study both. In argumentative writing we watched a Seinfeld episode—the one where Krammer loses his car in a parking garage and solutions are posed and not much resolved. I showed movie clips and asked the students what it reminded them of. "Of course it does!" I usually answered. Because we're humans and all stories are about human nature. Why not have fun connecting the dots?

I tried to pay attention to the problems other teachers were having and then find just the right assignment to address that problem. "Students delay and write their essays the night before," one colleague told me.

Yep, this I already knew. I've even had students brag about it: "Hey, Professor Pierce, whipped this out last night over three Red Bulls and a taco." Every time I will respond back, in teacher's red ink, "Looks like you whipped this out last night over three Red Bulls and a taco—the taco I guessed at only because of the salsa on page three."

Writing is a process of revision. You write and rewrite. Eventually you abandon the work. If you're in an academic program, you turn in the work for a grade. So I had an idea. My supervisor told me we didn't have to give a final exam—but I could if I wanted to. So I decided to. But how about something different? A teachable moment they'll never forget. How about a one sentence exam? Or, better yet, how about a *one word* exam?

The one thing I wanted my students to learn that semester was that writing is about revision—you do not get a written message right on the first try. *No way! No how!* I don't care what John Kerouac says. So on the first day of the new semester I began to set up for the final exam. I entered the room and before I even introduced myself, cleared my throat, or maybe cleaned my glasses, I wrote on the board, "Writing is rewriting." And I left it at that.

Then every day I wrote the same thing. The routine got to be a joke. The students would, in chorus, recite "writing is rewriting," as if it were a homily. The day before the final exam we reviewed the whole semester from day one. I filled the board with compositional wisdom. On the day of the final I entered the room with my satchel heavy on my shoulder. I emptied it of reams of paper—mostly blank, but they didn't know that and the expressions on their faces were priceless (in a sadistic sort of way, I admit). I plopped the reams onto the desk and they landed with a resounding *thud*. Then I approached the board and began to write, "Writing is ——————." I drew a long, inquisitive line, then turned to the classroom and said, "Fill in the blank. Put your name on your paper and turn it in and you're finished." The class fell silent.

"You're serious?" Someone asked.

One student, who had a good fifty pounds on me, raised his hand. "Yes, Dale?"

"I have one question."

"Yes?"

"Do you have a problem with a grown man giving you a hug?"

I threw open my arms and Dale hopped out of his chair and scooped me off the ground.

I did that same thing for about four semesters. One day, walking across campus, one of my students, a Navy veteran in his thirties, called out my name and waved. I waved back. "Writing is rewriting!" he called and flashed a thumbs up. He'd been a student of mine two years before. The message—the lesson—was in his brain and hadn't been scooped out yet, and he was able to shout it across the campus, spreading the knowledge.

I taught a two-week mystery writing course at a Christian college up North—twice. Always in January. I told the students they didn't have to write about a murder. "Just a hint of a crime is all that's necessary," I instructed them. All twelve still chose to write about murder. One student professed she had some help "offing" her victim. Her dad was a pharmacist and so she called him late at night and asked, "What over-the-counter product would kill a person?"

I froze in the warm classroom that stood on the snow-laden campus. "You did tell him what we're doing, didn't you?"

"Oh, yeah. At first he was freaked out. Then he called me ten minutes later and gave me another great killer. Then fifteen minutes later he said, 'Oh, this one is really good.'" She grinned. "I think I'm going to be okay with my murder." They were a good bunch. And although they sometimes made me nervous, we came away with some good mysteries.

I've taught writing workshops across the country. I've led men in rehab—*that* close to going to prison—to write about specific moments in their lives, and then listened to them read their stories, stories of a life before the "wheels came off," as they choked back tears. I've mentored a retired engineer who wanted to write a science fiction story about time travel and a woman astronaut who flew three shuttle missions. ("You've been in outer space!" I kept telling her.)

Not long ago I took a job in Bowling Green, Kentucky, teaching composition and literature. The university was about a hundred miles from my front porch in Tennessee. I'd rise about 4:30 each morning and drive north. So every day I crossed the state line and read about the bluegrass of Kentucky and how it's a great place to live. (On the way back I read about how wonderful it is to be a Volunteer and live in Tennessee.) Also at the state line, the people of Kentucky have installed one of those giant over-the-road marquees that remind all drivers to buckle up because "X" number of people have been killed on Kentucky highways this year. When I started the semester teaching at Western Kentucky University in September, almost 350 people had lost their lives on the Kentucky highways that year, a very sobering number. What was even more sobering was that every day I'd watch that number change—always going up, of course. Up five more today. Seven. Only three, that's not so bad, I would think. But each increment represented one whole life. Why can't they announce how many acres of bluegrass have been sown instead? Toward the end of November the number was up to almost 700.

At mile seventeen there is an identical marquee. One day between mile one and seventeen the number rose by two. "Stop it!" I yelled at the marquee.

One morning I pulled into the rest stop, like I usually did because interstate rest stops are always so big and clean and friendly—and well lit. I stood shoulder-to-shoulder with one fellow at the urinal. Then again with the same fellow at the sinks. Once again at the automatic hand dryers. On the way out, and to the car, I found myself in lockstep with him once more. It was awkward and someone had to say something. He chose to: "Finally a hand dryer that works," he said.

I agreed. "It's like they put a jet engine in those things," I told him. He nodded as we walked. "Yeah, really blows you away."

It was my turn to nod as we walked.

"Of course," he added, "Good old paper towels are just fine also."

I barked a nostalgic laugh and said, "Can't beat a good paper towel." Where was that car of mine? "You have a good day," I told him as I peeled off and climbed into my car. As I exited the rest stop I pulled beneath that monstrous marquee that told me three more people had lost their lives since this time the day before. I double-checked my seat belt and prayed a silent prayer that my "rest stop friend" had indeed completely dried his hands—even if was just on the backs of his pant legs—so that he could better grip the wheel and stay out of the bluegrass. At mile seventeen the number hadn't changed, so I figured he was okay, at least for now.

And then I thought about Bob back on campus, about his "tests." Had everything gone okay? Would I have to carry those heavy lesson plans into his classroom and break the news to his students? If so, I decided what I would do: rip up that handwritten syllabus and toss it into the air. I would announce how Jim's not with us any longer and his last wish was to skip over the annotation of T. S. Eliot's "J. Alfred Prufrock" that was due for today and instead pick up some fried chicken and head over to the funeral home. They would cheer him. They would cheer me. And why not? In the words of another one of my colleagues— also a college English professor: "It's your class. You can do whatever in the world you want to do—as long as it's not illegal." Good words. And I think encouraging college freshmen to skip a poem and go to the funeral home is not illegal. A good teacher is always looking for one of those "teachable moments." And this appeared to be one of those. Teach them to celebrate a life lived.

But that great lesson plan was not to be. Bob received a great report and is very much alive.

And so am I.

⁓

From our birthday, until we die,
is but the winking of an eye.

—William Butler Yeats

⁓

And in the end, it's not the years in your
life that count. It's the life in your years.

—Abraham Lincoln

⁓

12

"Happy Birthday to _____"

Back when I was alive, when I was sixteen, I was king of the world for a couple of reasons: one, I got my driver's license that day, and two, I had four girlfriends—the four prettiest girls in the Beta Club. I fancied they were my girlfriends because they each asked if they could ride with me to the Beta Club Banquet that night—in *my* car, with me and my new driver's license. I said yes to each one, imagining that none knew about any other car mate. But first I had to get my license.

In Ashland City, Tennessee, where I lived at the time on May 1, 1976, the driver's test was pretty simple. Dad told me where to find the testing center in the court house on the square. "They'll probably make you drive around town and then parallel park," he said. I'd never paralleled parked before. I worried about that. And I was worried even more so because my car didn't have a left turn signal. The year before, Dad had bought a 1962 Plymouth Valiant at a junkyard for $50. Then he bought a radiator and some seats that would fit and some decent tires from the same place and he and my uncle put it all together and the thing ran great. It was an automatic, but it had the pushbutton gear controls on the dash. I practiced for hours driving up and down the graveled road I lived on, until the woman who lived in the trailer at the end of the road ran me off with a broom because I was stirring up too much dust.

Because of the no left turn signal, Dad talked his boss into letting me use his truck for the test. I'd never driven a truck before. And this was one of those monster trucks where I sat up two car heights from everyone else and could look down on the roofs of cars. I was sixteen, 5'9", and barely weighed a hundred pounds. This would be like trying to parallel park a house.

A man with a clipboard followed me out to the truck. We climbed in and I adjusted all the mirrors, making sure he saw me and my thoroughness. I was so glad the engine started when I cranked it—mainly because I wasn't exactly sure I was even in the right truck. I put the truck in reverse and pulled out from the angled parking spot and drove to the main road. "Turn left here," the instructor said. This would have been embarrassing in the Valiant, without the turn signal. I did. "Turn left here," he said again when we got to the next block, to the street that ran by the side of the courthouse. "Turn left here," he said once more when we approached the street that ran behind the courthouse. "Another left here," he said when were at the street that ran down the other side of the courthouse, the one where we'd started. After every turn he'd mark something on his clipboard. "And finally . . . left here." We were back in front of the courthouse after driving in one big square. "Okay," he said, scanning the parking lot where we'd begun. "Just slide into that spot right there."

"The angled spot?" I asked.

"Yeah, that'll do." He checked something on his clipboard.

David W. Pierce

"No parallel parking?" Not sure why I brought it up. Mainly because I didn't want to have to come back because someone down the line, the someone who checks what it is he could possibly be writing on his clipboard, would sound off that I'd missed the most valuable part of the testing and I'd have to come back, that my license would be invalid.

But the instructor shook his head. "Nah. I've seen enough. Just angle it in there." He pointed the end of his pencil to an empty slot. I did as he said and he scribbled something at the bottom of the page. We climbed down from the truck and I took the paperwork to another part of the courthouse, took an eye exam ("I'm pretty sure that middle color is supposed to be yellow," I told the administrator of the test, "because it looks like a traffic light, but it's a *very* faded yellow. This must be an old test." I wasn't being smart; I just wanted them to know I had the eyes of an eagle.) They took my picture and I lied and told them I was 112 pounds. And just like that—after waiting for the glossy lamination—I was a licensed driver. I had just enough time to shower up, pull on the leisure suit my dad had bought me (it was dark brown and I wore a silky patterned shirt with a giant collar that came outside the jacket and a pair of platform shoes, which almost made me six foot), and drove off in my Valiant to pick up the girls—all four of them.

We met in the parking lot of the high school. The girls were stunning! Carol, Kathy, Laura, and Meg. All dressed in long dresses with high heels and their hair combed and ribboned up in ways I'd never seen them before in school. And none of them seemed to mind the old car seats that only a few months before had been in an old Chevy in a junkyard. The drive to Nashville was about twenty-five miles. Once we were loaded in, with me surrounded by yards and yards of the finest fabric, enveloped in at least four different perfumes (and my solitary cologne), and giggles and sweet, soft voices, I pushed the "D" button on the Valiant and made a right turn out of the parking lot.

About two miles from the high school, at the bottom of a long hill, a truck was turning. So cars slowed and stopped. There were four vehicles in front of me and three behind me. In my rearview mirror I could see Kathy and Meg and Laura, and I could see cars moving down the hill, slowing—except for this one car. Three cars back a single car swerved into the left lane, going way too fast. I could see the face of the driver. She was frightened. Her mouth was open in mid-scream. Her right arm pinned a child to the seat. She yanked on the steering wheel and sent the car into the left lane, missing the three cars behind me. Then she yanked on the wheel the other way and angled her car right into the left rear of mine—into the rear light that didn't work anyway.

The crash was loud. The girls screamed. I screamed. When I looked back, I could see blood streaming from Kathy's nose. Meg's upper lip was red and swollen. Blood was splattered on three of the four dresses. We piled out of the car. All those already stopped stepped out too. A quick search for tissue brought in enough that we could stop the bleeding. The mom who had hit me was rattled, but she was fine and so was her daughter. She admitted that she hadn't been paying attention and how odd it was that she'd completely missed the three cars behind me and only smashed into mine. Yes, very odd.

The officer who asked for my license said I looked taller than 5'9". I pointed to my shoes and he nodded. "And it's your birthday? Happy birthday! Just got this today, huh?" He waggled my license before returning it and gave me a copy of the accident report.

"Happy birthday, David," Kathy said, a wad of red tissue pressed to her nose.

"Habby birfday," Meg said, her lip scary swollen now.

"Your car appears to be okay," the officer said. "Of course, you won't be able to make a left turn signal. Be cautious of that. Other than that, you're good to go."

The girls stuck with me, even though some of the cars that had stopped were with our group and they could have divided up. They sang happy birthday to me—muffled and nasal and a bit off key. No matter how we may complain, we all love to have "Happy Birthday" sung to us.

And no one complained when I had to roll the window down to make a left turn signal. One of the teachers told the girls that if they soak their dresses in cold water, the blood should come right out.

Yeah, I was alive back then. Very much so.

When I was a zombie, I spent my forty-ninth birthday in a Nicaraguan jungle eating Mahi Mahi prepared by a culinary cook from the states at a place called Casa Iguana, owned by a man from Idaho.

I was off on another SCUBA trip with my buddies—Ken Evans, Steve Roos, and Bill Davis. A new guy came with us this time, Dave Rykard, but he fell ill that first day and spent most of it alone. We took turns checking on him throughout the day to make sure he was still alive, or needed another dose of Pepto Bismal.

I'd told the boys earlier that it was my birthday and they did what guys do: rapped me on the shoulder, told me happy birthday, guessed me to be at least ten years older, offered to help me up the stairs—things like that. Then we headed out to the ocean floor just off the coast of Little Corn Island, where we swam (and touched) long nurse sharks, felt uneasy at the close-up detail of the barracuda, and marveled at a jelly-like squid that kicked its tentacles through the water only a couple of feet from my nose.

Getting to Little Corn Island had been simple enough, but a long day of traveling. I had met the boys in Houston at 7:30 the morning before. We took a three-hour flight to Managua. Then we took an hour flight east from there to Big Corn Island, after a two-hour wait, where we had lunch (and Dave was pretty sure that's when he picked up the food poisoning). Once we got to Big Corn Island, we took a cab to the water taxi, which was a thirty-foot boat with enough seats for about fifty people. The seas were choppy that afternoon and we pounded across the top of the breaks for about thirty minutes before reaching Little Corn Island—population five hundred. No cars, no roads, no hot water. We did stay at a place that had air conditioning, but the electricity would go off every morning at 5:30 and then the room would heat up like a sauna, so you had to get out of there.

And once the electric shut down, I could hear the roosters crowing and the hammers banging. The residents on Little Corn are mostly fishermen, mostly of lobsters. We were there just before the season started, so much of the down time was spent building new traps. Traps were stacked all over the place. Beautiful rectangular boxes made from strips of dark cypress wood. Elegant-looking boxes, I thought. The old traps were weathered and gray. One of the workers told us a good trap will last about two seasons. I wanted to bring one home and make a table out of it, but I was sure it wouldn't fit in the carry-on bin.

So we heard about this place called Casa Iguana, on the other side of the island. We hiked there—about a mile away—for pancakes and eggs and coffee that could remove paint. We asked what would be on the menu for dinner. "Whatever we catch today," the owner told us. Can't get much fresher than that. So that night we took our flashlights and followed the signs back through the jungle. The path wended through a canopy of giant, leafy trees in whose branches in the daytime I had seen spiders as big as mice weaving intricate webs. This night we focused on the path in front of us—not the spiders or iguanas or other living, crawling things out in the jungle.

We heard the music long before we could see the place. Then we saw a glow of lights through the trees and heard the hum of a generator.

Surprisingly, the place out there in the middle of the jungle was quite busy this night. The owner welcomed us in and told us Mahi Mahi would be served very soon. We were instructed to pick a table and make ourselves at home. At our long table was a couple from Sydney, Australia. He was a former policeman there and now teaches people how to rappel off of buildings. "So that's your job?" I asked. "You get paid to rappel down buildings in Australia?" He nodded and seemed a bit embarrassed to have such a cool job. They said they'd been traveling through this part of the world for the last month. "So you're heading home this week?" I asked.

"Oh, no," the man answered. "We'll be out for about a year." I wondered who would teach the Australians to rappel off buildings while he was gone.

We ate almond encrusted Mahi Mahi with our new Australian friends and three girls at the end of the table who were from Switzerland. Later, our diving guides joined us—one from Sweden and one from England. The owner was from Idaho. My friends are from South Carolina, and I'm from Tennessee. I was just marveling at this melting pot here on the edge of the tiny island in Nicaragua, in the jungle, when desert was served—small sweet cakes that melted in your mouth. Everyone received a small cake except me. Then the owner from Idaho appeared carrying a cake before him—along with a single candle in a jar.

"We have a birthday boy!" he announced. He placed the cake and candle before me and began to sing—and all joined in. An international choir began to sing happy birthday to me. I could only smile. I pointed at my buddies as a way to blame them for this—as if I hated the moment. Then I braced myself for that awkward moment I knew was coming, when we get to the part where everyone has to sing my name: "Happy birthday dear_____." In crowds where people don't have a clue who the person is, there is usually some muttering at this point or, worse, just silence while the single person who does know tries to out-volume the muttering. But all I heard was my name—loud and clear—even from the Swiss. Someone must have laid some ground work.

I thanked everyone and then leaned over and blew out the candle. Everyone clapped and that part was done.

"Did you make a wish?" It was one of the Swiss girls.

I hadn't made a wish, but that would be embarrassing to admit that now. So I lied. "Yes, yes I did."

She bought it and everyone else seemed to also. As the conversations took off again, I stared at the cake for a moment. At the candle, as smoke swirled in the tiny jar. I can still make a wish and then everything will be back on track, I thought. But I couldn't think of anything—*not a single thing*—to wish for. Instead, I was thankful. I was thankful for Ken for bringing me with him on this trip. I was thankful for Bill and Steve and the way they giggled when my cake and candle came out from the kitchen. I was thankful for the Australians, the Swiss, the Swede, the Englishman, and the man from Idaho. I was a thankful man from Tennessee in the jungles of Nicaragua that night.

Still not a wish. But better. I'd much rather be thankful than wishful.

The jungle was full of life that night, and it had nothing to do with spiders or iguanas.

David W. Pierce

∽

Let us endeavor to live so that when we come to die even the undertaker will be sorry.

—Mark Twain

∽

What I want my friends and family to say at my funeral: "Hey, I think I saw him move! He's still alive!"

—Ken Davis, comedian, average golfer, and good friend

∽

13

Nothing Like a Good Funeral . . .

Back when I was alive, I went to a remarkable funeral. The deceased was my grandmother, and I hadn't seen her in years because our family was broken, estranged, and no one seemed to connect at any level—there, I said it. She was ninety-five and died like she was supposed to. The day was difficult on my mom and I felt bad for her for that. Because there was little organization, the funeral home director asked me, while I sat twenty feet from the casket on the day of viewing, if I would be a pallbearer. "Of course," I said. They also asked my brother and two of my two cousins, whom I hadn't seen since they were children. They were in their thirties now, grown up, hardened, in possession of cell phones and with girlfriends who had tattoos.

The minister who performed the ceremony hadn't known my grandmother. He did a great job of explaining the difference between the living and the dead and the rewards and punishments that come to those who die without knowing Jesus and those who do know Jesus. I was pretty sure the takeaway here was that grandmother (Granny) knew Jesus. If nothing else happened that day, it'd been a grand day. But we still had to get her to the cemetery.

My brother John, three years younger, had also been asked to be a pallbearer. After the short service, we exited through the employee's door to the back loading dock. My brother was still teary. He dabbed his eyes and I was moved at his tenderness. A director in a dark suite told us the casket was on the way and that we would lift and place it into the hearse in just a moment. Then a cell phone rang. It wasn't mine. My brother re-wiped his eyes with the back of his hand. My cousin Louie flipped open his phone and said, "Hello?"

Just then my grandmother's casket nosed its way into the lane we'd created. I took hold of one of the smooth metal bars that framed each side, that screamed to be grasped. I lifted and pulled. My brother on the other side did the same. Louie answered his phone, but one hand was still free for grasping.

"Hello?"

We pulled the casket along. Louie passed the weight of my grandmother forward and said, "Where are you, man?" I found out later that he was talking to his brother, my other cousin.

Pass, pass.

"Yeah, well, we're pall bearing up right now." *Pass, pass.* "We'll just meet you at the cemetery."

We settled Granny into the hearse. My brother's tears dried up. Since we'd loaded her up with a skeleton crew, I was wondering why we even needed my other cousin at the cemetery. We were more than capable. And Louie proved his leadership once the car stopped and we were all in position: "Okay, let's keep her head going this way," he said, as he grasped the bar of the casket and led us over the uneven, grassy lawn.

We got Granny to the right spot. The winches lowered her down. The smell of fresh earth will always remind me of young tomatoes and my grandmother's funeral. My mom gave me a big hug. Louie, now that his job was done, disappeared. I held my mother, and decided that I would do so all day if that was what she needed.

Yeah, I was alive then, very much so.

When I was a zombie, one day in the middle of Kentucky, I learned a valuable lesson: not everything that looks like a funeral is a funeral.

I was at a bookstore in Louisville doing a book signing about two weeks after the release date of *Don't Let Me Go*. There were several firsts involved here that day. One, it was my first book. Two, it was my first out-of-town signing. I'd done one already, but it'd been in my hometown and lots of friends had showed up, even though I had bought lots of sandwiches and expensive coffees to bribe them to come. Some I even threatened. The ones I'd threatened did caper about the edges of the store, but at least they'd come to show their support. But this was different. No one knew me in this town, and I knew no one.

I arrived a little early so I could meet the manager. His name was Doug and he was quite thorough. He'd set up an eight-foot table at the front door, covered it with a cloth and clipped a sign of my name and picture to the front of it. On the table were forty-four books, twenty-two on each side, geometrically stacked, much like Jenga blocks. A row of bookmarks and press releases spanned the front part of the table and connected the two stacks of books. Right after I got there, Doug ran to the back of the store and brought back two new Sharpies for signing and a bottle of water. He told me there was another bottle in the back, but he'd leave it back there for now to keep it cold. I was set and ready for two hours of signing my name and possibly presenting some witty comments that would pop into my head at the moment the pen touched the paper. I cracked my fingers, even though people have told me that could lead to early arthritis.

There seemed to be quite a few people there for a Saturday morning and I debated as to whether I should amble through the store and let those already there know that I'd arrived or just wait until they circled back to the front of the store. I opted to wait, to sit with my chin propped on my fists that clutched a pen, one that I could click again and again—like writers do. *Click-click. Click-click.*

The checkout was about fifty feet to the right of me. After a while I noticed that after people checked out, they'd make a straight line to the front door and they always seemed to be occupied with checking the receipt or wrestling a wallet into their pocket or peeking into their shopping bags, probably to make sure they'd gotten everything. They weren't looking at me, at me in full writer pose. *Click, click.* What to do? I decided to hold my pose and study the surroundings to see why this wasn't working.

Hanging in the window was part of the answer. A poster six times larger than the one on the front of my table touted *Really Woolly*—a product line of gift cards and stuffed sheep that convey the "wooliness" of ourselves and how Jesus still loves us. A cool idea and tough to work against. Another poster, about the same size, advertised a new vacation Bible study curriculum: *Boomerang Express.* How to compete with an adventure across Australia, complete with a travel trunk? And of course there were the Bibles. I saw at least five Bibles sold while I absently clicked my pen. One couple passed by and I heard the husband ask, "So what is it you're looking for?" I held my breath. *Click, click.* Maybe she'd glance this way and say, "You know something like that—a book about a father who climbed mountains with his daughter." Instead she turned to her husband and said, with a certain tone of exasperation, "I told you, a crown of thorns. If we can't find it here, then we have to go somewhere else." A crown of thorns. Really?

One pre-Easter shopper asked the clerk where the Easter cards were. When she told him they were sold out, he turned on his heels and blew past my table. I heard him say, "Out of Easter cards? Jeeze!" They'll have more in three days! I wanted to shout, wanted to joke. In my head it was funny, but I feared it would take too much exegesis for a bookstore encounter.

Across the street was a car lot and they were having a big sale. I knew this because they had one of those twenty-five foot balloon men that moved at the whim of the giant blow dryer hooked to its right heel, causing the purple, green, and yellow man to contort sometimes in what appeared to be painful positions, sometimes disturbing. I wondered if it was causing people to decide to buy a car that day, at that place. I wondered if I might borrow it for my last hour, or start thinking about getting one of my own. Would a twenty-five-foot purple and green man flailing with reckless abandon help me sell more books? Help me sell at least *one* book?

There weren't many families coming in. I was hopeful for young parents with children, especially daughters—like the family who entered with about a half hour to go. They passed by twice, but they would not look at me. On the third pass I spoke up, "So how old are you?" I asked the little girl. She told me four. "Oh, my little girl used to be four." Her daddy grinned and led her away, probably before I could push the hard sell on his daughter. She told her mom and dad, "I want a coloring book, with markers!" So she led them back into the store. A few moments later they returned, she with her nose stuck in the new coloring book. I couldn't let them get away. "That was easy," I said. Dad seemed to speed up, scuttling his daughter before her like one of those curling blocks you can see once every four years at the winter Olympics. To his back I warned him, "Just wait until she wants to climb a mountain!" I heard him grunt, but he never turned back. He pressed on, as if his greatest concern was to get his daughter home so she could color.

With ten minutes to go before I was sure the funeral dirge would begin, a rather large man approached the table. I'd seen him ambling about the store for the last half hour. I told him what the book was about. I gave him a couple of bookmarks. He seemed interested. I gave him a carabineer, one of the cool promotional pieces my publisher had given to me. It was the first time all day that I'd had a chance to offer one. He took it happily. Then he lifted a book from the table and read the back cover. "Let me go see what the wife wants to do," he said, and he took the book and disappeared into the aisles. While he was gone I straightened the bookmarks that didn't need straightening. Soon the man with the free carabineer returned, holding my book pinched between his thumb and forefinger, as if it were a kitten. He settled it back into the stand where he'd found it as he explained, "I guess we'll have to do this later." I thanked him and told him to check out the Website that was on the *free carabineer that I'd just given him*(!).

As I packed up, one of the store clerks came over and asked if I'd signed "any books at all?" I shook my head. "We'll, I sold one yesterday," she told me. I gave her a carabineer. Then the manager stopped by to tell me he was leaving. "So you're a biker?" I asked, pointing to his jacket with the big word "Harley" stitched across the front. We talked about bikes and he showed me some photos he had on his cell phone of a trip he'd taken out west. I told him I was thinking about taking some lessons. So he gave me some advice that may one day save my life. He told me to ride like I'm invisible. "People don't see you. They'll be looking right at you when they run over you." And watch out for sand or gravel on the road. For that, I gave him a carabineer.

I had a big box of carabineers under one arm when another clerk stopped me. He shook my hand and told me he had majored in English in college and wanted to be a writer. "So how'd you do it?" he asked me, waving a hand over the stacked books. I told him how I've loved writing since I was a kid. That I've always wanted to be a writer. I told him about working on the high school paper, the college paper, for magazines, and had written books that no one else wanted, books that someone might still want, and ultimately one that did find a home. He beamed like a child to whom I'd just explained where a cache of free toys could be found—even though I cautioned that it might take some hard work to get there.

"That's what I want to do," he said. I didn't give him a carabineer (actually I'd given Doug enough to give to everyone, so I like to think he wound up with one.) Instead, I offered him my hand. We shook and I wished him the best of luck. He couldn't stop beaming. He wanted to be a writer and I—with my unused Sharpies, and the undisturbed Jenga-stacked books that collected a day's worth of dust—had inspired him once again.

It was a long two hours, but a great ten minutes.

If I can inspire someone, I must be alive.

~

My roommate got a pet elephant.
Then it got lost. It's in the apartment somewhere.

—Steven Wright

~

14

The Lost Boy

Back when I was alive, the police showed up at my front door with a letter that pretty much said I was in trouble—or that at least David Pierce was. I wasn't there at the time but Chera and Zach were and they took the letter and wondered for many long minutes about what sort of trouble their father was in. The letter instructed me to come to the police station and ask for Officer Warren. "What'd you do, Dad?" Zachary asked me. I shrugged and searched my memory for any past traffic violations. Maybe there was a bill I'd forgotten to pay. Were there long periods of time that I couldn't explain? Was it possible I'd robbed a bank in my sleep?

"I'll just run downtown and clear this up," I said, still holding the letter open and before me, trying to read between the lines.

"I'm coming with you," Chonda said. She grabbed her purse and then gave me a look, one that seemed to bore into my forehead. On the way out the door she said, "So you don't know what this is about, huh?" I shrugged against the pressure of the seatbelts.

At the police station Officer Warren had us sit at a round table. At least we were in what looked like a break room and not one of those interrogation rooms with the one-way glass. He was tall and slim, maybe in his fifties, with jet-black hair combed back. When I showed him my letter he pulled out some paperwork of his own housed in a manila folder. "Let's see," he said, reading from the open folder. "Have you ever lived in Texas?"

Instantly I felt relief. The answer was no. I told him so and was about to stand to leave.

"How about the town of Drummond?"

I thought for a minute. I don't know why I hesitated. I'd never heard of Drummond. Suddenly I got the feeling this hesitation was going to be something he would use against me later. "No," I said and shook my head. "Is that in Texas? Because I've never lived in Texas." I thought that should cover any other questions regarding Texas.

He kept reading from the folder. "Do you know a woman named Sally Walton?"

Chonda had been focused on Officer Warren, but at the mention of a "Sally," I saw in my peripheral that her head swiveled, so that she was now looking at me. I felt stabs of heat coming from that direction. "No, I don't know a Sally Walton. Does she live in Texas? Because I've never been to Texas. What's this about anyway?" Officer Warren took a deep breath and laid the folder on the table and turned it so I could read it. Chonda leaned in close. "We're looking for a David Pierce who owes some back child support." Officer Warren looked at me, kind of stony-like. His lips were pressed tight together and he seemed to be pushing spit around with his tongue, like maybe he had a bad taste that wouldn't go away. I got the feeling he had no respect whatsoever for a deadbeat dad.

"Well, obviously, you've got the wrong guy," I said, trying to sound casual. I suddenly had the feeling that if I was in one of those interrogation rooms, I'd be taking nervous, quick glances at the mirror.

"We were in Dallas once," Chonda told him. Then she looked at me, "Remember?"

Why did she say that? I looked back at Officer Warren. Still stony. Something in his mouth moved from right cheek to left cheek. "That's Dallas," I said, my voice rising. "Yeah, we passed through. *In the airport.* I've never even been in the city. Besides, he's asking if I've ever lived there—in Drummond." That was for Chonda.

Officer Warren turned the folder back so he could read it and asked, "You are David Pierce, right?"

"Yes, but I'm not *that* David Pierce. My middle name is Wayne. Does it say what the middle name is?" I waved a hand at the folder.

"No middle name," Officer Warren said. "There is a social security number, though."

When he told me what it was, I laughed (short and still nervous). "Well there you go." I raised both hands in a nothing-to-hide gesture, which is the same as a the-defense-rests gesture. "That's not my number."

Chonda said, as if Officer Warren wasn't even there, as if my testimony about the social security number hadn't just killed his whole case, "Did you ever go through Texas on your way to a writer's conference?"

"I don't have a wife and kids in Texas," I told her. I realized what that sounded like and added, "Or anywhere." I realized what that sounded like and added, "Except right here . . . with you and the kids. . . ."

Officer Warren rubbed his chin thoughtfully as he kept picking pieces of evidence from the folder. "Says here you are six-foot three."

"*That* David Pierce," I stabbed a finger in the direction of the accusatory manila folder, "is six-foot-three." I stood. "Look, I'm barely five foot." (I'm five-foot-nine, but the truth was not working as a good defense for me.)

Officer Warren looked me up and down. He looked at the folder. He looked back at me. Finally, he said, "Huh," and closed the folder. I heard Chonda exhale. "We must be looking for a different David Pierce." He stood and shook my hand and then led us to the exit.

"I hope you get your man," I told him. I got the sense he was making mental notes of me, my description, in case my name ever came across the wire again and he was asked to describe me to a police sketch artist.

On the way to the car, still in the parking lot, Chonda said, "If you ever leave me and the kids, I'll kill you."

Oh yes, I was alive then. Very much so. But if I had ever lived in Drummond, Texas, had a different social security number, and was about six inches taller, I'm pretty sure she would have killed me that day.

As a zombie, a most curious letter lay on my desk for several days. I could have gotten rid of it long before, especially since there was nothing in it that pertained to me. But I kept the letter anyway. I even kept the envelope because at the lower left-hand corner in bold blue print and all caps were the words "MISSING PERSONS BUREAU."

The letter came from The Salvation Army and was addressed to me, but not really. A woman I'll call Bonnie Crump was searching for a man named David Wayne Pierce, who was born in 1960 in Tarboro, North Carolina. I was born in the same year but in Nashville, so I couldn't help her. The letter was very polite and offered an 800-number. It was the subtext that broke my heart: "It has been some time since she has last heard from the relative being sought and would like to do so."

I folded the letter, returned it to its envelope, and stacked it with bills and other correspondence that needed attention. I tossed a Stanley

David W. Pierce

Steamer coupon for a rug cleaning and had the letter right there, hovering just above the trash bin. But I placed it back on the counter. On one trip, back to my office, I picked up the letter and brought it to my desk. Now the letter was opened so that when I sat next to my keyboard I could read it. The juxtaposition of my name on the front of the envelope next to MISSING PERSONS BUREAU raised a thin, shadowy doubt: What if I *am* the one Bonnie Crump is looking for?

I should be answering e-mail or paying bills or watering the potted flowers on the deck. Instead I read the letter again. "It has been a long time since she has last heard. . . ." What had happened? How did she lose this other David Wayne Pierce? Was it an accident? Did she take him to shop at Sears one day and he got caught up in the crowd and swept away into another life? Or did she give him away? That sounds more likely. Perhaps in 1960 Bonnie was a young woman—a girl really. And along came a child that she couldn't take care of. So she ran the new baby over to the Tarboro Orphanage and left him on the front steps. But before she left she threw a rock through the upstairs window so he wouldn't be outside for too long. She always did have a good arm. But the baby had a slight intestinal problem and this made him cry all the time so no one adopts him. He spent the next seventeen years in the orphanage, most of the time on kitchen duty. Then, just before his eighteenth year, when he could legally walk out, he escaped from the orphanage and hitched a ride on a bus with a double-A baseball team. Turned out he was a natural at baseball. He made the team and hit homeruns all the time. So he changed his name to Cal Ripken and got lost in the big leagues. Bonnie's always been a big baseball fan and watches the All Star game every year. For nineteen years in a row she watched him play and always thought there was something familiar about the way he threw a baseball.

Maybe that's what happened.

151

Maybe he was kidnapped by pirates. Maybe Tarboro, North Carolina, is close to the ocean. (Not really. I just looked it up so that story won't work.)

What if she was not exactly *missing* him. What if she *needed* him—after all these years. Perhaps she hit the sauce pretty hard, after losing him and all. Only now she had straightened out her act and was working a good twelve-step program. She was at step four now: make amends to those you've hurt. She figured losing someone must have hurt him in some way. So she was retracing her steps, hoping to make amends.

Or maybe she needed a kidney?

What if she was filthy rich and about to die and has no one to leave her money to?

I called mom and asked her if she knew anything about Tarboro, North Carolina. "Isn't that near the ocean?" she asked.

I looked through old family photographs. There are three children in my family. I have one brother and one sister. We all look like little clones of Mom and Dad. Just then Zachary walked in to see what I was doing. "Working," I told him. He picked up a sword I'd bought in a yard sale when I was twelve. He pulled it from its sheath and sliced the air in front of him. He made grunting sounds, battle sounds. He fought pirates. He fought bad guys who were storming the castle. In less than a minute he had saved the day. Then he sheathed the sword and returned it back to its resting place against the wall and walked out. I suddenly felt safer and resumed my work.

MISSING PERSONS BUREAU.

We had a bureau when I was growing up. It was an old piece of furniture that Dad got from his mom and dad after they passed away. It was huge. As big as a refrigerator. When we first got it Dad laid it on its back in the garage and brushed on stripper to remove all the old varnish. Then he stained it and replaced all the knobs with new ones.

"It's solid cherry," he told us. That alone was supposed to convey to us kids how precious and valuable that old bureau was—even though we didn't understand at that time. There were five drawers and I could lay out in any one of them at the time. A bureau that big could hold a lot of stuff. It could hold thousands of the same kind of letter I'd just received. I wondered how big the MISSING PERSONS BUREAU is.

I had to put this letter away, but before I did, I saw at the bottom there was a reference number: 7228. I was tempted to write just to see if Bonnie Crump was making any progress, to give her my e-mail, and ask her to drop me a line with any news. Maybe she had a blog I could follow. I wondered if David Wayne Pierce from Tarboro, North Carolina, was even still alive.

As far as I know anyone who wants to find me can find me. I don't have a reference number. I don't have a bureau searching for me. I can imagine a new identity. I can wonder about what happened. Where did things go wrong? Will there be a reunion sometime soon? Some things I'll never know the answer to. But what I'm certain of is this: that I am right here now—and alive.

I finished for the time being and put the computer to sleep. On the way out of my office I picked up the sword, slowly unsheathed it and, with a flick of my wrist, cleaved the last scoundrel that lay waiting in hiding behind the bookcase—a piece of furniture as big as a bureau. There is something to be said about not being lost.

~

We must love one another, or die.

—W. H. Auden, American poet

~

The tears happen. Endure, grieve, and move on.
The only person who is with us our entire life is ourself.
Be ALIVE while you are alive.

—George Carlin, comedian

~

15

Zombies Can't Swim

Back when I was alive, I thought I was going to die. But I did do a foolish thing when I chased after that drifting boat.

I was fourteen years old, and we lived in a house next to a lake. There is no greater life for a fourteen-year-old boy who loves to fish and swim and thinks of himself as another Huckleberry Finn. The boat belonged to a neighbor. It was a simple, metal, flat-bottom boat and, after paddling around all morning and visiting all my favorite honey-holes (that's lake-talk for where the fish are), I beached the boat at our yard, but I must have forgotten to tie it up. Mom spotted it first and said something like, "Hey, that boat's drifting off!" I ran the length of the yard and then waded in up to my chest but couldn't reach the boat. Huck Finn would just swim out to it. So that's what I decided to do.

I swam for about a minute, making nice long strokes and slicing through the water like an Olympian. Afraid I would bump into the boat, I stopped and treaded water and saw that the boat was still several yards out. *Hmm?* So I swam some more. When I stopped again, I still found myself a long ways off. The wind was pushing that flat-bottomed boat as if it were a sail. I looked back and saw that Mom had followed me down to the water. She had waded in up to her waist and was asking if I was okay. "Almost there!" I called back. I swam farther on in the direction of the boat. When I stopped again, I was *still* too far from the boat. And now I was too far from the bank. And I was tired. I wasn't as strong a swimmer as I believed I was. Huck Finn would have been disappointed in me.

Mom was calling something from the bank but I couldn't tell what. My ears were roaring and I was treading too hard to stay afloat. The boat kept drifting. I went under to rest my arms for a moment. But the effort to surface and start up again seemed to double the exhaustion. That's when I made peace with God. Since I was only fourteen, I covered all my sins in about two leg kicks. So I talked to myself: "So this is how it all ends? I heard drowning is sort of like sleeping. It's not too messy, especially if they can drag my body out soon—before it can swell up and turn all purple. I hate that Mom has to see this, though. This will be hard for her. Therefore, I shouldn't flail about too much. If I do that, she'll have nightmares for the rest of her life! She might even try to swim out here to save me and drown, too. The neighbors could be watching and that would give *them* nightmares—to witness a double-drowning. So I should just go quietly. I should just slip under and pretend I'm going to sleep. That first breath (or no-breath, really) will be the toughest. Soon. Soon. My arms can't keep going. . . . What was that?" Something floated by and nearly hit me. White, like an angel. Floating, like a savior. It was a milk jug, bobbing like a cork, within arm's reach. I raised a limp arm and corralled the jug against my chest and went totally limp, as I would on a pillow, thankful that someone had finished off the last of this milk not too long ago, most likely. Thankful that someone had taken out the trash not too long ago, most likely. And thankful that someone had gone to the trouble to screw the cap back on, most definitely.

I could hear Mom now, above the sound of my own breathing. I don't think she could see the milk jug. No doubt she was marveling at my swimming strength. "I'm good," I called back in a winded breath. And I felt good mainly for her. "Almost there!" I called.

I found strength to kick myself over to the boat. I climbed up its metal side and came out of the water. I lay on the flat bottom of that boat, very Huck-Finnish, I thought, with the sun on my face, holding the milk jug as close as a lover, feeling new and very much alive.

Yeah, I was alive then. Very much so.

As a zombie, I went diving again with the boys. And I looked forward to this trip more than any other, probably because I was teaching three literature classes and two composition classes at Western Kentucky University and commuting about two hundred miles round trip every day. I was six weeks into the semester and my head was fuzzy with other people's prose. I needed to be with the boys again, to hear the jokes they'd robbed from the Internet and laugh until we sufficiently annoyed the people at the table next to us, to be underwater where I could only hear myself breathing and feel the breath roll up the sides of my face in wobbly air bubbles. That's what I needed.

Ken set everything up—tickets, dates, times. I met the boys (Ken, Steve, and Bill) in Houston (they came from South Carolina, I from Tennessee) and barely made the connection to Panama—the country. After the four-hour flight, we took a tiny plane for about another hour to the island of Bocas del Toro. There's a dive shop there called La Buga. (You'll recognize it by the reclining tree frog painted on the building's exterior.)

The diving wasn't so remarkable. We'd dived in better places and had seen more spectacular sights. Here the water was murky and the fish were hidden. But the coral was plentiful and kaleidoscopic—sometimes passing as an endless, frameless water coloring. It was on our third dive when our very young dive master took us to a sight and said, as we suited up, "Okay, I've never been at this site before. But what do you say we just jump in and see what's down there?" Not a one of us questioned that. I guess we all hoped we were about to get a little slice of "danger." Or, maybe, no one wanted to sound like an alarmist—or worse, afraid.

But this dive was like the first two: murky and uneventful.

Our fourth dive of the second day (eighth dive total) is the one that got a bit "uncomfortable." I would say scary, but since Ken, Bill, and Steve may read this later and draw the wrong conclusions, I'll just say "uncomfortable." This was the dive Bill and I rode the sausage to the surface, and not exactly because we wanted to either. But first let me back up to dive number seven—where this "uncomfortable-ness" began. I'll get to the sausage thing later.

It was about 3:30 in the afternoon and we'd had lunch and were ready for our third dive of the day—the seventh in two days. The boat dropped the four of us and our guide, a young woman named Freda—who looked to be twelve—to the site. Before we went down she told us there were some surges that we would have to kick through, but it shouldn't be a problem. I was doing my best to keep up, fighting these surges, when we came to a cutout in a wall that made a deep, green, vertical trough. Freda turned and pounded a fist into an open palm—like she would if she were cracking a nut. Then she pirouetted back and kicked across the trough. I took this sign to mean that we would have to kick hard to get through this. That on the other side was rest. Or maybe walnuts.

So I kicked like a kangaroo in a sack. I got through this trough, only there was no rest, so I grabbed hold of a rock and held on as the surge tried its best to pull me loose. When I looked back, Bill was doing the same, but Ken and Steve . . . *were just gone*. In diving, if you get separated, the rule is to search for one minute, then make your way to the surface. Our guide didn't seem too alarmed. I squeezed the rock tighter. But I was longing for the surface myself.

Bill and I held fast for some long moments, and then Freda led us onward. There was a cave to the left and she pointed inside—to indicate that there was something worth seeing in there.

While I hung on to a rock, Bill kicked into the cave. He held his camera before him, presenting one poor shield against whatever might be in there. I could only see the tips of his blue fins that peeked out and flinched every so often. Then the fins took long, deliberate movements and I could tell he was trying to back out. A coffee-colored cloud rose like a giant mushroom around him. In another second or two I knew I would lose sight of the blue fins completely. If he was ready to come out, I would help him. I grabbed hold of one of fins and gave it a good tug and Bill came out—breech birthed—from the clouded cave.

When he saw me he gave me the okay sign and we kicked on into the surge, following after our fastly disappearing guide. Slightly above us, and to our left, we spotted Ken and Steve! They'd found us. Steve swam to me. On the previous dives he'd made it a practice to breathe off my tank for about five minutes. Since he used more air than any of us, this allowed us to stay down longer. He checked my gauges and shook his head. He looked in the direction of the dive master, who had disappeared, then sliced the water with an open hand in the other direction, indicating that we should swim that way—go *with* the current.

All in me went limp, and I sensed the same had happened in the others as well. No more hard kicks, hanging onto rocks and coral for rest. We simply went slack and let the current take us. Steve unrolled a lift bag—a bright fluorescent orange nylon bag—and pulled out enough string, then inflated the bag with his air hose. The bag shot to the surface many feet above us and we drifted along with it for another five minutes. The orange bag on the surface was the equivalent of jumping up and down and screaming, "Over here! We're over here!"

As we drifted along, burning no calories now, breathing only enough to keep our hearts beating and our brains alive, we took the time to marvel at life. Steve found a large flat rock and turned it over, hanging onto our lifeline with the other hand, stirring the sandy bottom and watching for tiny sea creatures. Bill found a perfect sand dollar and cupped it in both hands and shared it with Ken.

After a few minutes of just drifting along, we grouped up closer and began our ascent. We stopped at fifteen feet from the surface for a routine safety stop—to allow the built-up nitrogen to dispel from our bloodstreams. We floated and hung suspended, like four drowned people, just below the surface. Finally, our five minutes were up and Steve gave us the okay sign followed by a thumbs up, which means "go to the surface." I exhaled and thousands of exploding bubbles swarmed about my head like bees, and I followed them. The surface above me was a sparkling, textured plate of glass that the sun played on. With a lifted hand I broke through this plane to the hum of the ocean, the steady hum of life, with the orange lift bag bobbing like a cork beside me, and Steve saying, "What was that all about?"

I petted the rowdy surface of the ocean, as if it were a giant water pet.

That steady hum of life was broken only by the sound of a boat motor growing closer.

An hour later, on the next dive, Bill and I got swept away and couldn't find anyone.

The surge had been so strong this time that for almost thirty minutes I crawled along the ocean floor, only about twenty-five feet down, pulling along the bottom, clawing, and at one point using my dive computer and compass like an ice ax, stabbing it into the beautiful, living coral—so what if it may have taken a generation to form! —and hoisting myself along. The indigo blues and emerald green living corals ceased to be awe inspiring. No more comparisons to kaleidoscopes or watercolors. Now they were rude, harsh, garish, and even seemed to be mocking me: *we can breathe and you can't.* I could, but it was becoming increasingly difficult.

Fan coral flapped in my direction with each surge. The dainty and fragile fans seemed to shove me back with superhuman (or rather, super-plant) power. I spotted a sandy spot just to my right. Up ahead I could see Bill's bright blue fins in the murk. What if I just lay in that sand a moment? I thought. Like a big nurse shark? Get cozy there on the bottom and rest? Earlier we'd found a nurse shark, at least six feet long, wedged under a rock. Bill got up close and took its picture. Then he swam to the shark's tail and gave it a wiggle, then a jostle, a pull, and, because the shark hadn't budged yet (and all we really wanted was to witness its stately form as it glided through the currents), Bill gave it one big *yank.* The shark bolted out and we *ahhed* through our mouthpieces. Later, our guide told us it'd been asleep. Now, clawing along the bottom, tired, breathless, and nearly lost, I could understand the sleeping part. The sand was smooth and appeared soft and mattress-like. Wiggle into a niche between the sand and a rock, I thought, and just rest. That would be nice. Just then Bill yanked on my arm, and I bolted back and pulled my gauges out of the coral.

He wanted to check my air level. I had 1000 pounds left. You're supposed to be on the boat with no less than 600. Bill let me know he had 650. "Let's go up," I signed back with a thumbs up. "I'm tired." There is no sign for tired. I just slumped my shoulders and tried to look sleepy.

Bill pointed in the direction behind us—down current. We spun around, tucked our legs, and let the ocean sweep us along. *Ahhh,* the rest was nice. Bill un-pocketed his floatation safety device, much like the one Steve had used the dive before. Sometimes it's referred to as a sausage because of its sausage-like shape. It is an orange fluorescent, six-foot tube that needs air to float.

The other half of this safety device is a spool of string with a clip on one end. Bill clipped the sausage to the string. Together, while drifting far from our guides and deeper into the blue, we found the valve on the sausage. Bill undid a hose from his vest and shot the tube with air.

Before the sausage rose, I wasn't feeling too good about the physics of it all. We were at thirty feet down and, with its fresh breath, the six-foot sausage, in an incredibly galvanic moment, took off to the surface like the space shuttle. Bill couldn't unspool the string fast enough. I tried to let the string brake through my palms, but instead the sausage yanked us both up with it. We shot from thirty feet to about five feet in seconds—not good. If we surfaced too fast we could have gotten decompression sickness, the bends, an excruciatingly painful and even life-threatening result of too much nitrogen in the bloodstream. But once the sausage was on the surface, we quickly sank back to the desired fifteen feet and dangled there for the next five minutes.

Once it was safe to go to the surface, I went first while Bill cranked in the slack string. The dive boat had spotted the sausage and was there waiting for us. The only people in the boat were the two dive masters (*hmm . . .?*). "Are you by yourself?" she asked, as I removed my mouthpiece and mask to breathe as much of the free air as I wanted, as was possible.

I scanned the surface. Bill's air roiled up next to me. He was on his way. "No," I answered. And suddenly the gravity of this answer, greater than that of the water's hold on me, that kept me from lifting off into the sky like an inflatable sausage, tugged on me hard as I added, *"Bill's with me."*

We found Ken and Steve bobbing along about a mile away.

That night we ate fish that had swam in the same waters with us only hours before, and Bill and Steve told joke after joke and we laughed so much that people stared at us, envious of our laughter, I was certain. Envious of the life that seemed too large to be spilling out from only four people. But we'd been baptized—*twice*—that day. We'd come up for the air and all the life. But that comes with that.

And that was more than our dinner could do. Something was happening to the zombie—something significant.

⌒

I feel so alive
For the very first time
I can't deny you
I feel so alive
I feel so alive.

—P.O.D., Christian metal band

⌒

It is extreme evil to depart from
the company of the living before you die.

—Seneca, first-century Roman philosopher and humorist

⌒

A Typewriter and the Japanese Golfers

Back when I was alive, I taught myself how to type. It happened during the summer between my sophomore and junior year in high school. I worked on the school newspaper then, writing a sports column. I would interview some of our hero athletes and engage in hyperbole that had our football team on the verge of turning into a pro franchise. But the coaches loved it and I liked to imagine that if ever I were cornered by bullies (or even one bully), the whole offensive line would come pimp-walking around the corner, with smoke roiling up from nowhere, backlit so you couldn't make out their faces. One silhouette would call out my name and ask if I was having trouble. The mass would be moving toward me, glacier-like, overshadowing the bullies. "You wouldn't be causing any problem with our little writer friend, now would you?" And the bully would soil his pants, then flee, and the team would circle around me and one of them would ask, "So what are you going to write about us this week? How strong we are? Unstoppable? That we have bionic legs?"

And so I would write these columns in long hand, pass them off to our staff typist, who would often question me, saying things like, "Can Scott Tooley really bench press the team bus? Sounds far-fetched to me." "So let me get this straight, Art Glasgow passed a football from here to the square? That's three miles."

Which would always lead me to say, "Just type it, okay?"

"Maybe you should take typing next semester," our sponsor, Ms. Cooper said. But that was a whole semester. I still needed Latin to get into college.

I had a better idea. "Don't they have a textbook?" I asked. They— the typing department—did. "Then I'll just teach myself. That is, if I can borrow one of these babies." I laid a hand on an IBM Selectric. Top of the line. There was a ball the size of a jawbreaker in the center of the machine, exposed, with raised lettering circling about it like alphabet barnacles—complete with all the punctuation marks and such. With one push of a button, that ball would spin and snap against the page and leave its impression. I'd try as hard as I could to watch the process, to pick the letter out, its spot on the silver-colored ball, and watch it spin and snap into place, but the process was just too fast. The whole machine must have weighed forty pounds. But Ms. Cooper agreed and I lugged it into the back of my Vega, along with a textbook, and drove it home for the summer. This is the summer I would teach myself to type.

The summer before I had taught myself to juggle. I took three tennis balls and practiced in the front yard for hours on end. It took about a week. The first five days was nothing more than throw them up, grasp in the air madly, pick them up from the ground, and start over. About day six the balls seemed to float and all I had to do was pluck them from the air and send them off to their next spot in the rotation. On the seventh day I rested.

I didn't think typing would be so easy.

I parked the Selectric on a table by the front door in the trailer where Dad and I lived—only six feet from the air conditioner that made our little trailer feel and smell like an Artic swamp (if there is such a place). I opened the text book to chapter one, used a heavy glass ashtray to hold it open, and began to learn. QWERTY threw me that first day—what that even meant—but then I caught on and soon settled in on the home row. Without even lifting a finger, I learned to type seven letters and a semi-colon that first day. Only nineteen letters to go! And although the exercises were loaded with incredible amounts of repetition, I couldn't imagine why the book should be so long.

When Dad was gone I could kill the air conditioning and kick open the front door that would allow a humid blanket of heat to envelop me. *Click. Click. Click.*

When Dad came home, he liked to cool things down. He'd crank the air down as low as it would go. An icy jet stream would pass above my head and fall like a snow blanket on my shoulders. My pinky fingers would be the first to suffer. Atrophied as they already were, it became increasingly difficult to maintain my p's and q's. But little by little my pinkies grew in strength and dexterity with every punch of the q, p, z, and ?. (And even though I didn't think I'd be using the q and z so much, I gave them equal training time.) This is how children in Alaska must learn to type, I thought. They set their Selectrics up against one side of the igloo and skate along the home row.

I discovered I loved the forefinger letters (like J, F, Y, and T), and I would pound them unnecessarily harder—just because I could. And I was glad to read that I was allowed to double up on some letters using these same two fingers. TYBNVMRU quickly became my favorites. Once I added the other vowels—E, I, and O—whole words began to eke out from this forty pounds of steel and ink.

Dad told me that all typists could type the phrase—and without looking—"Now is the time for all good men to come to the aid of their country." Don't know why. Those are easy words. Easy letters. I gave it a try and did it. And Dad gave me one of those professorial nods and would probably tell his buddies later how he helped create a break-through moment for me and my typing. "Until that moment," he would probably tell his friends, "he was just typing qwerty over and over again."

But my typing experience still didn't feel quite complete. The summer was nearly over when I once again bent the book back and weighted it open with the ashtray to a page that suggested I try "The quick brown fox jumped over the lazy dog." So I tried it, and I did it. And like the juggling balls on day six, my fingers found their respective spots and suddenly I was typing. *Clickity, click, click.* And that was with the air conditioning on. Kick open the door and bring in the humidity and it was more like *click, click, clickity, click, click.*

I realized the reason this typing textbook was so long was because there were still all those punctuation marks to contend with and things like @ (really, how often would I ever need that in the future?), #, $, %, ^, &, *, and parenthesis, brackets, hyphens, and quote marks. I did invest a great deal of time into the shift and tab keys. But I still had to glance at the backspace. So just before my junior year of high school started, I made the call to skip *all* the numbers and symbols. If neces-sary, I would just cheat and look at the keyboard. Besides, my ears were in the early stages of frostbite.

I lugged the typewriter back to school and was told I could keep the textbook, since they would be getting new ones this year. I tucked it away on a shelf somewhere, thinking maybe one day I might get back to it.

I typed lots of stories in high school, mostly about our football team (we won five games my junior year and lost six, but my stories were the equivalent of the overly exuberant fan who has a camera swung into his face and his first reaction is to raise a foam finger and chant "We're number one!"), about the too tall speed bumps that often stranded students for days with no food or water, about a skateboarder who jumped over cars long before that was cool. My nose was always to the ground, looking for the next story, so I could write it, then pound it out on the keyboard. If there were any questions about my story, they came from the editor and not the typist, who may have had incredible ampersand skills, but knew nothing about that inverted pyramid of who, what, when, where, and how.

When I entered the university, my typing skills were useful on the college paper, where I was paid four cents per square inch of published story. I'd clip my works out and collect them each month, some with bylines and some without, and turn them in. It was a good way to make five or six extra dollars a month. But more than that, I now possessed a skill that could pay me money. I wanted to get better. To write more. I just didn't know what. All I'd written so far was for school assignments or school newspapers. I was on the police beat at the university, which sounds interesting, but it required, at times, I interview the officers. It was too tempting for me to take something like, "We apprehended the suspect at 23:48," and write "And just before midnight, as the villagers slept on a blanket of assumption of complete safety, we wrestled the beggar to the ground. Tommy put a knee in his kidney, and I had him by the Adam's apple—just daring him to spit one more time." The editor usually frowned at the license I took.

But that's what I wanted to write. Rather than talk to someone about what really happened, I realized I'd rather make things up. So my senior year in college I began a novel, a fantasy complete with castles and giants and littler furry creatures that were startlingly similar to Ewoks—long before Ewoks had ever been thought up. I talked my advisor into letting me complete my novel for my senior project. He did, and so, in the evenings and on weekends when the office of the apartment complex was closed, I'd use their IBM Selectric. Only since this was a fantasy story, I thought it'd be cool if it were written in script. I saved my money and bought a replacement ball for the Selectric. Each day I'd replace the standard font with my script tool. For me it was a crystal ball—containing all the letters needed to write all the great stories the world would ever need. At the end of the day I'd take my script ball back to my apartment, contemplating which letters would be used next, and in what order.

Not long after I graduated, I married. And not long after I married, we had a beautiful daughter. Since fixing things—like toilets and air conditioners—and typing were all I knew how to do, I kept fixing things because repairing leaky toilets paid more than typing the next great American novel.

Our daughter was about a year old when I got a job offer that could potentially change our lives forever. A friend of mine introduced me to a company that trained nursing home administrators. "We're always going to have old people to take care of," he told me. It was the most logical thing I'd heard, maybe ever. So I took the job. It meant packing up the family (that word "family" was still so fresh to me) and moving about an hour and a half away, from Nashville to Glasgow, Kentucky. It also meant taking a $1,200 loan to buy some suits and ties that I'd need for my new white-collar job. We found a small house to rent and convinced the owner to allow us to tear up the old carpet to expose the hardwood floors beneath because the previous occupants had had a dog problem, or a cat problem, or maybe both. They may have even used the living room as a staging area for that earlier ark trip—that famous one.

At first the job was interesting, even fun, although I felt somewhat self-conscious wearing a coat and tie to work every day. The key was to appear as if I'd always worn a tie to work. But because I wasn't sure how to do that, I'd adjust the knot every so often—to let others know that I was aware of my dress and always have been and always will be. When I fixed toilets, I got to roll up my sleeves. Here, I just wiggled my knot.

The idea of the training program was to run me through all different departments, from financing to nursing. By the time I was finished with the eighteen-month program, I would know the nursing home business inside and out. No better place to start than with accounts payable. And no better way to approach accounts payable than with old accounts payable that needed to be filed. "Take these old invoices," one of the office workers explained to me, waggling a single yellow piece of paper, "and match it with the cancelled check, staple them together, and then file it away in the proper vendor folder. Try to keep them organized by the date. Oldest in the back."

Sorting. Filing. Numbers.

"I can type," I told her. But my typing services were not needed that day—or for many, many days.

Another part of my training involved finding creative ways to positively reconcile the accounts receivables. In other words, how to get payment from those who owed us money. I was given a long list of names with phone numbers and how much was owed and the last time they were contacted and how many total times they were contacted.

I started with the ones who'd been contacted numerous times with no results. I'd get results, I thought. I'd straighten out this little company-that-could. For hours I got nothing but answering machines or endless rings. They were on to us.

Here was a new one. Contacted twice before. Promised to send something, but hadn't yet. A man answered after a couple of rings. "Y'ello."

"Mr. Armstrong?"

"Yes."

"I'm calling from Sunny Acres Nursing Home." I paused for him to say something like, "Well, I be dern. Good hearin' from you again." But instead there was just silence. "I'm showing you still have a good-sized outstanding balance here." More silence. "I'm calling today to ask if you could possibly send some money along and we can begin to take care of this debt."

I paused again and just when I was sure he wasn't going to say anything he spoke: "That was momma."

"I'm sorry. Who was momma?"

"That was momma who was there. She died about two months ago." He drew in a deep breath and said on the exhale, "I guess I could send a little something. We bring in the corn in a few weeks and I guess I could send more then."

I suddenly pictured him at his mother's funeral. Maybe he wore overalls and a white Sunday shirt. I imagined him singing "Amazing Grace" and his voice breaking up each time before he could get to the end of each verse. I imagined him and his wife later, adding up columns of numbers on a sheet of paper. The left column would be headed WHAT WE'LL MAKE ON CORN THIS YEAR. And the right column headed WHAT WE'LL SPEND ON CORN MONEY THIS YEAR. The left column would be short and sparse and easy to understand. The right column would be filled with items like flour, salt, grain, seed, shoes, and momma's feeding tubes.

I didn't like this part of the job. I thanked him and asked him to do what he could. I wrote by his name "Will send money soon." Then I returned to the list and tried to pick those older names, the ones I figured would have an answering machine.

Because I offered my typing skills so much, I suppose people eventually learned I liked to write. "I wrote a novel," I said one day, with a new list of phone numbers before me, along with names and how much money each owed us. "Really? What's it about?" And so instead of calling grieving corn farmers, I'd tell my colleagues about Dandril, a commoner who falls in love with Arielle, the castle's princess, and Brodansia, the giant.

Someone suggested I write a story for the Shady Acres Newsletter (didn't know they had one!). I could even do a story about Dan Lessenberry, they told me. "He's written a book, too," someone said. "He's sitting right over there," and this co-worker pointed across the lobby to a man in a wheelchair.

I'd never used the word *dapper* in my life before then. I'd heard of it, vaguely knew what it meant: someone British, dressed in tweed, bow-tie, hat. Mr. Lessenberry had none of these accoutrements, but immediately I believed him dapper. His hair was white and perfectly combed and trimmed. He sat straight, shoulders squared, wearing a white shirt buttoned at the neck and a pair of black driving gloves, to protect his hands from the chair's wheels, I guessed.

With pen and paper I approached Mr. Lessenberry. Someone told me he was nearly ninety. In the few weeks I'd been working there, I'd seen patients in all stages of disability—with bed pans, catheters, feeding tubes, diapers. You name it, you will see it there in a nursing home, probably in the hallway. What struck me was how clean and crisp looking his shirt was. Across the lobby, there was a urine puddle by a TV tuned to *The Price Is Right*. While someone else went after a mop, I knelt and introduced myself to Mr. Lessenberry and shook one of his gloved hands. The leather was soft and made me want to wear gloves all the time. He smiled as I told him who I was and what I was doing. He said he'd be glad to help.

"So you wrote a book?" I asked.

He smiled and nodded.

"Tell me about that."

"It was a textbook."

"Textbook?"

"It was the only one of its kind for thirty years." He smiled with a fond remembrance. "For thirty years I revised it and sold it to schools all over the country. There's good money in textbooks."

Since he'd brought it up . . . , "What kind of money?"

Very matter-of-factly he answered, "$100,000."

"Wow, that is a lot of money," I said, as any cub reporter probably would.

"For thirty years."

"$100,000 for thirty years?"

"For every year."

"$100,000 for thirty years, *every* year?"

He smiled the biggest and warmest yet and gave a nod to go along with it.

"So what's the book about?"

"Typing."

"Typing?"

"How to teach students to type. For thirty years. The only one of its kind."

"I think I have that book," I said. He just looked at me as if he probably got that a lot.

I finished the interview, but now I was anxious to get home. We still had some boxes stored in the garage, so I dug around, still in my dress shirt and tie, until I found the box of books I remembered packing. Somewhere near the bottom of this box, because it was a large book, was my typing manual. On the gray cover, beneath a sketch of a typewriter, was his name: D. D. Lessenberry (David Daniel).

Well, I'll be.

I wished I'd drug that book back there and had him autograph it. That would have been a better story.

But I didn't that day. And I wasn't there much longer after that. I was working at the office, billing patients for supplies—spit trays, peroxide, tape, lots of gauze (always lots of gauze). This was also the day my director told me that we needed more private-paying patients. "They really help the bottom line, which is something you will always have to think about when you're an administrator," she told me. "We need more private-paying patients like Mr. Lessenberry."

We had a bed open up recently, which was a euphemism for "another one just died." My director met a family at the front door, a man in overalls, with his wife and some high school-aged kids. They were looking for a place to bring the man's mother. He had his thumbs hitched in the bib of his overalls. The wife did most of the talking. I listened in as I billed for gauze.

"We finally decided we had to do this," the wife said.

"I'm so sorry," answered my director, "but we're full and I can't tell you when another bed will open. Have you tried Scottsville?"

"But that's an hour away. If we want to visit her every day we can't drive an hour away."

My director shook her head and I could read the "I'm truly sorry" expression on her face.

The wife talked more, as if talking about an empty bed might produce one. Maybe she believed the director would remember a quaint little bed she'd forgotten about just down the hallway by the kitchen.

Finally, the man spoke as he pushed out on his bib and said, "Is there any way at all?" He seemed to be gazing above the director's head, figuring something. I imagined he was guessing about when the corn would come in.

But the director just shrugged and said, "Scottsville."

The family left and that's when the director walked over to me and explained that they were Medicare people (that's how we tagged them). And that the bottom line stuff was all important right now. And that we could sure use a few more Mr. Lessenberrys. And that Scottsville wasn't that far away.

I was six months into this program, and I wasn't very happy with the nursing home business. I liked helping people when I could, but I didn't like *not* helping people when I could. I wanted to smile like Dan Lessenberry when I was ninety. I wanted to wear soft leather gloves and talk to people about my book(s). I wanted to write something that would change people's lives, even if they did pack it away in the garage later. I was twenty-four years old. I had a nine-month-old daughter. I had a wife who would wash out six diapers every day and more than once used tea towels until she could catch up. We scraped our pennies together every month. We had garage sales and sold things people had given to us as wedding gifts. Somehow my typing book got away from me, but not Mr. Lessenberry's warm smile.

We went back home to stay with family that weekend. On Sunday night, when we were supposed to drive back, I told my wife that I was quitting. I didn't think of it as quitting so much as turning around and getting off this path that would only drain me and take me further away from my dream. There is no warm smile in that direction, I determined. Nothing warm down there at all.

On Monday morning I called my director. She always seemed hard and intimidating. But not today. I felt emboldened by the new possibilities before me.

"Mrs. Kyle, it's David. I won't be coming in today."

"Okay. Need a day off? When will you be back? Tuesday?"

I couldn't believe how giddy I was feeling about what I was about to say. "You know what? I won't be coming back at all. I'm walking away from this. It's not for me."

Then she said something that confirmed I'd made the right decision. "Now, David, don't think you've failed just because of this. The nursing home business is not for everyone."

Seems we had different ideas about what success is. I told her I was happy with my decision and hung up. Then I went to look for a job.

I went back to repairing toilets and air conditioners. On my next birthday my wife bought me a typewriter—not an electric one, but it was smooth as silk. I was the maintenance man for an apartment complex where I took the typewriter to work and between jobs and on lunch break I'd write stories. There was no heat in the shop so in the winter my fingers would grow numb if I typed too long—just like they had in that small trailer when I found the home row keys for the first time. It was good to be back.

I was working and taking care of my family. I was pursuing my dream. I was not on an easy road (sometimes toilets go screwy at two in the morning), but I could sense I was not on the wrong road. I was determined to work hard, to be honest, and to write what was true—or rather *type* what was true. I felt alive again.

Like I said, I wished I'd had Mr. Lessenberry autograph that book. I wish it was here on my desk as a reminder of that change in direction. But maybe it's best I don't have that book. It's just a textbook about typing. And, after all, Mr. Lessenberry taught me way more than just how to type.

Yeah, I was alive then. Very much so.

As a zombie, one day I went golfing with some Japanese strangers. It'd been over thirty years since I'd learned to type. Since then I'd written short stories that were published in national publications, magazine articles, and even a couple of children's books. Only a few months before I'd sold my first book. It was about climbing mountains and running marathons with my daughter, recording my experiences from the front row seat I had of watching her grow into a young woman. The book was titled *Don't Let Me Go.*

These two strangers I'd met were engineers with the Nissan car manufacturing company and had been here the last few days. I connected with them for the round and we talked as best we could. Their English wasn't that great, but I think they understood more than they could speak.

On the second tee they asked me to take a picture of them, so I did as they posed on the tee box, each leaning on his club.

"So what do you do?" one asked me after I lucked in a birdie (a very rare occasion for me). "Play golf for living?" Then he paused (seconds later I would discover it was for comedic timing) before saying "... like *every* day?" They both laughed and took turns slapping one another on the back. I've always believed communicating a joke in another language must be incredibly satisfying, not to mention the greatest form of diplomacy.

On the third tee box I took another picture of them and again on the fourth, fifth, and sixth. At number four I began to shoot the photo at an angle that would at least include the tee box number somewhere in the background. I figured they'd thank me for that later.

"English?" they asked. "You teach English?" They seemed puzzled and exchanged confused looks.

"We have lots of people here who can't write with proper English," I told them. They nodded as if they could understand that.

"And you teach how to write?"

Yes. And then, I think because for the first time—because I could—I said, "I also write."

"What you write?" one asked.

"Lots of things. A book." That felt good.

"Book?" And their eyes brightened. "What's your book about?" They seemed way too interested. I had them move closer to the number nine tee box sign as I snapped their photo. Their pose changed very little from the previous seven photos.

"It's a story about climbing mountains with my daughter," I told them.

"Mountains?" And one of them waved a hand into the air to indicate a mountain, making sure he'd heard right, that he'd understood the word.

"With daughter?"

"Yes," they told me. And they told me that they each had young children at home.

"What's it called?" They were asking a lot of questions and we still had one more hole to play.

So I told them: "*Don't Let Me Go.*"

Simultaneously my two new Japanese friends rolled back on their heels, turned their heads up, and let out long guttural growls, the kind of sound a father will make when thinking about his little girl growing up and getting married and starting a family of her own. *That* kind of sound.

And just like that, with those four words and their groans, the ocean between us shrunk and my new friends and I were simply three fathers on a golf course with the same dreams, goals, and, I'm sure, fears.

"I will find book," one of them said to me, and then he repeated my name over and over again so as to memorize it. I couldn't help but think of Daniel Day Lewis in the movie *The Last of the Mohicans* when he tells his true love "I will find you!" There was nearly that much passion in his declaration.

Today I like to think that somewhere in Japan—perhaps next to a quaint koi pond shaded by a groomed bonsai tree—a father is reading about another father's adventure with his daughter. He may be groaning with recognition. He may be dabbing away a tear. He may be contemplating getting an ice cream cone later with his child—all because of the words I'd typed.

That makes me feel alive.

~

Come alive, come alive.

Come Alive, come alive.

—Mark Shultz, recording artist and champion of The Living

~

17

Swimming with Sharks

Back when I was alive, I swam with the sharks—and not meta-phorically either.

I'd only been certified to dive for a few months and had maybe half-a-dozen dives under my dive belt when my good friend and dive buddy Ken set us up for an afternoon at Stuart's Cove, where we would feed the sharks. We were on a family vacation with Ken and his wife Alison in the Bahamas. "You've got to do this at least once," he told me. Ken had been certified longer than me, maybe a year. But I still viewed him as the expert. He assured Chonda before our first dive together that he would take care of me. "Look," he told her, "if he dies down there then . . . I'll die too." Neither of us took much comfort in those words.

There were twelve of us on the boat, including our guide Pedro and photographer Lisa. While on the boat, Lisa gave us some simple instructions. "You guys go in first," she said as she pointed to the ten of us pulling on our wet suits and double-checking our air tanks. "It's about fifty feet to the bottom, very clear. Make a circle and rest there on your knees. Pedro will bring down the fish to feed the sharks." Pedro was at the front of the boat suiting up with chainmail—the kind you see King Arthur wearing during sword fights. "And I'll be taking lots of pictures. So smile!" Then she slipped some chain mail over *her* arms. The woman across from me had a knife strapped to her ankle. Suddenly, I coveted that knife. All I had was a rubber air hose. Even if I could beat a shark back with that, I wouldn't have any way to breathe. Pedro wiggled and the chainmail that enveloped his arms and chest rippled like a small ocean wave.

Neither Lisa nor Pedro had to tell us we were at the dive spot because we could tell by the sharks that circled our boat. Large triangular fins sliced the water as they made concentric circles around us. Just beneath the surface we could see them, and we made guesses: "That one's at least six foot! Oh my gosh! Eight foot. Look there!" The woman across from me rested her hand on the knife strapped to her ankle. Once again I coveted.

Lisa, very perky now, gave us further instructions. "Okay, now you guys go ahead to the bottom and circle up. We'll be there right away."

"Now?" someone asked (could have been me, *was* me). It seemed every moment we spent there, more sharks appeared, circling, roiling the waters, mocking us humans.

"Oh yes, now is perfect. Don't worry. They don't like human flesh. They like fish."

But wouldn't they have to taste me first to discover that I wasn't a fish?

"And oh," perky Lisa added, "make sure you put some extra weight in your vests so that you can keep still. Because if you tip over you don't want to do this," and she waved her hands in the air, paddling the air, as if to keep her balance. "Because the sharks will think your hand is a fish."

She smiled her perkiest smile yet and said, "See you on the bottom!" Her chainmail tinkled a happy tune.

So like lemmings, one by one we each stepped off the edge of the boat and into the circle of circling sharks.

Underwater they were bigger. Sleek. Graceful. Misunderstood. And all the other adjectives that are used on cable TV during "Shark Week." I sank as fast as I could, clearing my ears, watching for the woman with the knife in my peripheral, not really understanding why getting to the bottom would make me safe, unless it was because there was one less side I could be attacked from.

Lisa was right: it was very clear at fifty feet. Divers call that good visibility, or better, good viz. We had no problem seeing Pedro swoop in with a spear strapped around his chain-mailed torso and a wire basket of dead fish in his hands—trailed by at least a dozen reef sharks, none of them less than six feet long. He planted the basket in the center of our small circle then used the spear to bring one of the dead fish into the open, where it was immediately attacked by one of the sharks—shook and shredded and gobbled down. I thought the carnivore might even have belched. It should have. But we were underwater, so maybe not.

This action served only to bring in more sharks. They swarmed us. Maybe forty to fifty darted in and out of our circle, ripping dead fish from Pedro's spear, bumping our heads with their tails, fanning our faces with new ocean currents as they passed.

Lisa was there with us, working her camera so that once we got topside (if we ever got topside) we'd gladly pay for a photo of ourselves defying death. She was on her knees in the circle next to Pedro, pivoting about from one diver to the next. When she got to me, a shark grabbed hold of her flash and tugged it hard. Our usually chipper Lisa leaned back and gave the camera a giant tug and ripped the flash from the jaws of death. Then she repositioned herself in the sand and gave me a nod (and I'm sure a smile) to let me know it was my turn for the photo.

I tried to soak in every second, to see as much as I could. I swiveled and pivoted my head as much as a human vertebra would allow. A giant shark passed just to my left, sleek and shiny, with a rusty hook stuck in the corner of his mouth and at least eight feet of nylon string trailing behind. Somewhere on land, someone was telling the story of the one that got away. Here, I had found him. When I turned to look at Ken, he was stone still. No part of his body would ever be confused with a fish.

Another shark swam toward me, maybe the largest one yet, just over my head. I could have reached out and touched it if I hadn't been fearful of my hand resembling a fish. And there, only a foot from my head, the giant seemed to yawn. His mouth stretched open to three times the size of my head—including my mask. A row of razor-sharp teeth glistened and caused me to wince, until a second row of teeth pushed out, as sharp and glistening as the first. A foot above my head! I quickly made a deal with God, promised to be a missionary if need be. And then, there in the sand, on my knees, hands pinned against my body, I shivered, much like I do sometimes after I urinate.

When all the dead fish had been eaten and Pedro left with the basket, so did most of the sharks. We scrounged around on the bottom for a few moments and found some shark teeth we kept for souvenirs. Then we headed to the surface, slowly, cautiously marking the route of the remaining sharks that still circled us. Once I surfaced and kicked my way to the boat, I wondered if my foot might resemble a fish, and shivered once more as I crawled onto the boat.

Ken was already there, getting unsuited and doing all the other things you do after a dive—put a finger in your ear and waggle it vigorously, pinch one nostril and blow out the other, eat some candy (to counter the salt). I crawled up next to him and began the same routine. I'd just cleared the right nostril when Ken said, "I didn't know it was going to be like that." It almost sounded like an apology.

"What did you think 'Feed the Sharks' was going to be like?"

Ken shrugged and shook his head. "Not like that."

I thought about this on the ride back. So you sink to the bottom of the ocean. You drag along twenty pounds of dead fish and dole it out at the end of a spear to forty ravenous sharks. Only one word comes to mind: frenzy. And one phrase comes to mind after that: don't look like a fish.

I hadn't known what exactly to expect. But I hadn't been disappointed, and neither had I been shocked. "Feeding the sharks" is not equivalent to taking a stroll along the beach. The heart *should* speed up!

Now here we were—off the bottom of the ocean floor with loose shark teeth in our pockets and all *our* teeth in our heads. Twelve of us had commingled with the ocean's greatest predator (I know, I know it wasn't exactly the Great White), and we'd come out alive. The woman across from me never had reason to unsheathe her knife. (Why had she even carried it in the first place? What sort of a chance would she have had if that scenario had played out?) I leaned back against the fiberglass hull, feeling the vibration of the motor that precluded any small talk, happy to feel a breeze that cooled us from the heat and dried our clothes, nursing a Tootsie Pop, and sensing I was near the chocolate center.

We rode back together in silence, silent in our own thoughts, sinuses cleared, benefactors of a shared experience, and *alive*.

Yeah, I was alive then. Very much so.

As a zombie, I recently found myself surrounded by dead people, thousands of them. And I couldn't find my way out.

I was on summer break from teaching and had a few days before classes would start, so I wanted to visit my son who lives and goes to school in California—in West Hollywood. I knew he was taking summer classes and working part time, but I figured we'd whittle out a few hours of the day to do some fun things. I didn't realize how much free time I would have in that week, or that I would have to sleep on an inflatable mattress, or that I wouldn't have a car. But I've always liked to hike. In retrospect, hiking boots would have been great. Sneakers even better. But for this hike, flip flops would have to do.

So one morning, while Zach was off to school, I slipped on my flip flops and set out to see Hollywood, looking for a good story, I told myself. And I would begin with the cemetery. It was on the map I owned and appeared to be a big grassy area in the midst of a grid work of asphalt streets. Quaint, even. I hiked from his apartment down to Santa Monica Boulevard and turned left. But before that I stopped at a corner market and got a bottle of water. A man was returning a bottle of milk and a sandwich to the cooler as I walked in. He swapped them for a canned Coke that he waved at the attendant behind the counter, an older man who was balding and wearing glasses and the two top buttons of his shirt undone, and said, "Thank you."

The attendant turned to me and explained in broken English, "He has a card that we don't take. But," and here he sighed, "he's thirsty. It's only seventy-five cents."

After I paid for my water I slid an extra dollar across the counter. He seemed confused. "It's for the thirsty man," I told him and stepped out to continue my hike.

About halfway to the cemetery I met Larry. He was sitting on the ground, old boots on his feet, clothes disheveled, and reclining against a knapsack. "Gotta quarter?" he asked, squinting against the bright sky behind me.

I stopped and said, "How much do you need?"

"A quarter. See, I'm trying . . ." his voice trailed off as I reached into my pocket. Guess he figured I was going for the quarter and he didn't want to blow that.

I had four quarters and gave him all of them. He thanked me and smiled. Since I was in no hurry, I sat down next to him and immediately he sat up straighter, pushing off his knapsack. "What's your name?" I asked him.

"Larry."

I shook his hand and he explained that he was out of money and had a check coming in ten days. Then he pulled from his pocket about six different IDs—a medical one, driver's license, and others, but the one he pulled to the front to show me was some sort of military ID. In the photo he was younger, thinner, and clean-shaven. The street had beaten him down, I guessed. "I was in the Air Force," he said proudly. "Stationed in Berlin for six years."

He told me about his job as a clerk, ordering supplies for the men over there. Not so much a glamorous military career, a simple one really, but one he seemed to care about, of which he was proud. Now as a veteran he was getting a check, only he'd run out of money to pay for the motel where he'd been staying. He raised a hand and steadied it horizontally before him, as if to draw a line in the air. "I have to find a way to make my money last between checks." I could guess that the space above the line he drew was okay. He could survive. Below the line meant he would sleep on the street. "I tried to win some at the horse races, but blew that." His hand dropped way below the line, and he laughed like you do to keep from crying. Then he canted his head and narrowed his eyes and asked, "You ever live on the streets?" I told him no. "Well, it's not easy." He came across as an expert.

"So where will you sleep tonight?"

He looked up the street in one direction and then the other before saying, "Oh, somewhere around here, I'd say. I'll wait until it gets late. I don't worry about here." He mentioned another part of the city and said, "If I was over there, I'd be worried about getting my head bashed in. But not here." He smiled as if he were blessed.

When I left, I shook his hand again. Thanked him for his military service. I'd have given him more money, but I figured he'd hobble on down to the horse track and make another bad bet. Larry told me where to find that cemetery that I'd told him I was looking for. As I walked away I watched him recline back onto his knapsack, one that was hardly inflatable.

Hollywood Forever is the name of the place I was hiking to. On a map things always look closer. In real life it was 2.8 miles away. I arrived at the gate not long after I'd left Larry. El Pollo Loco and liquor stores gave way to a deep, lush greenery protected by an iron gate attached to a guard house. The gate had been swung open. I stepped up to the window of this house and asked if I was allowed to walk through and take a look around. "Oh yes, sir," the guard said, excitedly, as if he rarely got the chance to talk to living people. "We are open to the public." Maybe it was his contagious excitement that caused me to turn and step off the curb without looking and into the path of an oncoming car. I braked; the car braked. I waved a thank-you-for-not-running-me-over wave and scooted on across. Before I could even reach the opposing curb, however—and safety—I wondered if any of the thousands of people buried in that place had actually died *there*? I could have been the first! I could have possibly even made the cover of a new brochure, to replace the old black and white photo of Rudolph Valentino that was there now.

Once safe again, I turned right and followed a trail that wended through a commingling of grass, granite, and buildings. The buildings I quickly learned were mausoleums. I picked one at random and stepped into it and immediately had the sensation I'd had once when I stepped into a hall of mirrors. The ceiling was tall, thirty feet at least, and arched, the walls lined with bronze rectangular markers, each bearing a name, some dates, and maybe a short phrase—like "Beloved Husband, Brother, and Father." To the right and the left, on and on and on, as if the purpose of this spot was not to provide a resting spot for the beloved dead, but to create a space where potential art students could visit to learn about perspective, to witness the convergence of parallel lines as they extended farther and farther. I stayed there no more than a minute, until I was dizzy with depth, then stepped back out into the less symmetrical granite and grass.

And even though they meant nothing to me, I began to read the names and dates on the stones. I would do quick math and think something like, "Wow, a good, long life! Good for you!" or "Only twenty-six. I wonder what happened?"

I passed through what was marked as the Jewish section. Names I could not pronounce (and so many in Russian!), but the math was consistent. This one died old. That one died young. But they were all dead. Some of the newer graves had pictures on them. I imagined the family had riffled through all the old belongings, searching for a favorite likeness they could all agree upon.

Unlike driver's license photos, I believe all gravestone photos are excellent. The subject is usually smiling, or at least appearing erudite, but always so alive. It also always intrigued me to see the living, smiling images superimposed on a stone juxtaposed with the final date of life that was always carved into the stone.

And were the stones ever multi-racial! Some were old and weathered, some new and shiny and slick, some made of limestone and others of a granite that would make for a great kitchen countertop. Some were shaped like hearts and tree trunks, others arches and gateways. Some graves were topped with blooming flowers and ensconced by dwarf hedges. At times I would be bowled over by the brightness of some of the flowers, but more than once I discovered the source was not nature but rather cut and dyed silk—again, the dead among the living.

I never expected I'd ever see anyone I would know in this place, since I have no history in California. But I turned a corner to see the grave of someone I'd known of since I was a kid, watched him all the time on TV—Alfalfa of the "The Little Rascals"! I saw he died the year before I was born.

And there was a bronze statue of Johnny Ramone, who founded the rock group The Ramones. I've never been a fan of theirs, but I thought I might pretend to be later when I'd tell people about my trip. I was more interested in David White, who was Mr. Tate on *Bewitched*. And there was Don Adams from *Get Smart*. "Nearly missed you by that much," I told him as I walked on past, holding up a thumb and forefinger to pinch an inch of space. And there was Darrin McGavin. He played in lots of different shows, but my favorite was when he was Carl Kolcheck, who chased down vampires and werewolves in *Night Stalker*. That show always scared me when I was a kid, but in a fun way.

I saw almost no one who was alive there. A single man plucked dead blooms from a hibiscus plant. I watched him for a moment. He pulled a handful of the dead ones off, carried them across a pathway to a corner created by a wall and some tree roots and dropped them there, then returned to get more. I was interrupted from this by a crow, a large black crow/raven that hopped along between the stones. I stepped in its direction trying to make it fly away. To scoot. It only hopped farther away, disappearing behind stones, then reappearing in the open spaces. I teach English at the university in my hometown. "Really?" I said aloud and I remembered the man plucking dead hibiscus blooms and so lowered my voice. "Can there be a more clichéd symbol?" I took another step toward the bird and it took another hop. So I let my academic mind off the hook: maybe sometimes a crow is just a crow.

Then, almost in a sudden way, I was ready to go—only I couldn't find my way out. Hollywood Forever covers about a hundred acres. The stones, the pathways, and the mausoleums all conspire to create a labyrinth. I turned left and walked for a ways, then right and more walking. Same. Same. Same. Another left and I saw something new. Two large rectangular, stone boxes rested on stone pedestals, parallel with each other with rounded tops and long names carved on the endplates: Constance Adams DeMille and Cecil Blount (I always wondered what the B stood for) DeMille. I paused. A sense of awe at the life he must have lived settled over me. One of his most famous achievements was directing *The Ten Commandments*. I studied their gravesites. I turned and looked out over the endless sea of granite and limestone, knowing the exit gate was out there somewhere, then turned back to Cecil B. DeMille and, with an Old Testament weariness, said, "A little help, please?"

Without the aid of a miracle, I finally made it out of Hollywood Forever and continued on my way to a more festive area on Hollywood Boulevard. Here I expected to find movement and sound and energy— back to the land of the living. On the way there I spotted a bird perched on the corner of a seven story apartment building. I tracked him as I would the moon as I passed block after block. The bird never moved, never fluttered, never dove after a field mouse. Finally, I concluded it was a decoy, nailed down there on the corner perch to scare away those pesky pigeons.

I turned at the corner of Vine Street onto Hollywood Boulevard and immediately became distracted by the brass (gold-looking) stars imbedded in the walkway. Again I found myself reading the names of people, some living, but mostly dead. A man in his fifties had sat next to one of them as he squirted a bit of polish onto a cloth and buffed the star bearing the name of Montgomery Cliff. He wore knee pads like those of a carpet layer, his crutches stacked just to the side. I watched him work painstakingly at the edges of the star, magically wiping away the oxidation that had created a patina of darkness that threatened to obscure the name. I wondered why he cared.

I stopped by Grauman's Chinese Theatre, one of the first theaters in this town and one of its oldest landmarks, built in 1927. The large open area out front is spotted with concrete impressions of the hands that belonged to the stars—Marilyn Monroe, Frank Sinatra, Roy Rogers, and even his horse Trigger's shoes. Hordes of people walked in crooked directions, allowing names that attracted them the most to lead them from one set of prints to the next. Strangers constantly bumped into one another because they were so preoccupied with looking down. Someone was always having a picture snapped at a favorite spot, or placing their own hands in the solidified print. I wondered what sort of thoughts they entertained when they did that.

Across the street I spotted a hamburger place with lots of personality—The Pig'n Whistle, made of old, dark wood and bricks. Someone there told me it was the place where Judy Garland celebrated her sixteenth birthday, about the same time she was filming "that little movie" known as *The Wizard of Oz*. I've always been more of a fan of the scarecrow, but I wanted a good hamburger.

While working on my giant burger at a sidewalk table, I watched a young man with a checkerboard haircut work hard on the street, fanning brochures into the hot afternoon air that promised the best Hollywood tour in town. Mostly people ignored him, others waved him off. A guaranteed opportunity, for two hours, to view the houses of Lucille Ball, Elvis, Dr. Phil, and The Playboy Mansion were wasted on this bunch. I finished up, paid, and left the Pig'n Whistle and ran right into the checker-headed huckster. "Excuse me, sir," he began, the brochures were close to my face and extremely colorful. "Would you like to see the homes of the stars?" He hardly took a breath before launching into the rest of his spiel, one I'd heard at least seven times already from my lunch table.

I interrupted him somewhere around Dr. Phil's house with "Yes. Yes I would." I plucked a brochure from the fan of brochures and from the look on the young man's face, you'd have thought I'd just made a triple jump on his game-board head and was due a crowned king.

A few moments later I sat in a van that'd had the top removed for better viewing, along with a father and son from Germany, two college boys from Switzerland, and a family of four from Indiana. Our guide's name was Kent. He was in his thirties, a movie buff (nut is the word he used), and an actor who would soon be seen on a world-wide release on DVD—a horror film he said.

Kent had curly, cropped hair and wore a gentleman's hat decorated with a plaid pattern. He used a microphone so we could hear quite easily. First he drove us close to the Hollywood sign and explained to us that in the beginning it had been a very, very cheap advertisement for a new subdivision located at the foot of that mountain in 1923 known as Hollywoodland. In the fifties the city voted to keep the first nine letters, and in the late seventies they replaced them with something more durable than plywood. The letters are forty feet high and fifteen feet wide and at one time were lighted around the edges with 4,000 light bulbs. There had even existed once an old cabin behind the sign where, for years, a man lived alone and his sole job was to replace the burned-out bulbs. I couldn't help but think about that man and his job for the rest of the tour. *How'd he climb up? Did he carry the bulbs in his pockets? Did he ever drop any?*

"And here we are circling Lucille Ball's home. . . ."

What wattage were they?

"To our left Frank Sinatra once called this his home for. . . ."

Did he make daily trips to the hardware store or were they shipped in?

"If you look above those trees on your left, right above that mini-van, you'll see the roofline of the Playboy Mansion. . . ."

Did his own little cabin have bulbs that were burned out and he never got around to replacing them?

". . . of Cher and Elton John. . . ."

Did he ever climb down from the top of that O (any of the three) and, once back on the ground, notice a new one out right next to the one he'd just replaced?

I thought of the old man on crutches who polished the brass stars that dotted the walkway along Hollywood Boulevard. How much polish did he use a day? A week? A year?

I was only able to stop thinking about the light bulb changer when our tour guide suddenly grew melodramatic (now I could picture him in that horror movie). We pulled up at a nondescript iron gate sided by hedges that hid everything behind them. Kent told us that beyond that gate had been the residence that Michael Jackson had rented as he practiced for his last tour, the one that never happened.

"And across the street, ladies and gentlemen, behind that gate," Kent's voice boomed and he pivoted as if he sat on a ball bearing, "is where Elvis and Pricilla lived." He pivoted in the opposite direction and pointed to the first gate. "Over there, the King of Pop. Over there," another pivot and point, "the King of Rock and Roll. And who did the King of Pop marry?" A long pause followed this question, but I was sure that everyone—even the Swedes who seemed to speak little English—believed it to be a rhetorical one. So Kent answered his own question: "The King of Rock'n Roll's daughter, Lisa Marie." I was waiting for a musical cue, but Kent only settled back behind his wheel and our van eased around the corner. We stopped after only a few feet. Our guide hovered over the wheel, his back to us for a long moment, before turning around again, this time much slower and he seemed to anchor himself by clasping his seat back. No more pivoting, his body language said.

"Now, ladies and gentlemen," he said, almost stoic now, nearly spent of energy. "If you'll look back over your shoulders, I'd like to draw your attention to that plain brown, wooden door above the hedges there." I looked and saw the door, fronted by a small balcony. Kent continued: "It was behind *that* brown door that Michael Jackson received a large dose of propofol. It was behind *that* brown door," he was a bit louder this time, "that Michael Jackson slipped into a coma. It was behind *that* brown door" (was he turning up the volume on purpose?) "where Michael Jackson, for all practical purposes, slipped away from this world!" Then he dropped the volume when he added, "And we lost the King of Pop that day." Kent froze with his eyes piercing the air space above our heads and in direct line with the brown door above the hedges, frozen there for some time like a period at the end of a sentence. Soon Kent slowly turned and settled back behind the wheel, and without another word we pulled away. It took every ounce of control in me not to shout out, "Then for crying out loud! Won't someone *paint* that door?"

The man who worked at the market and gave away cold drinks to thirsty people. Larry from the Air Force who loved ordering basic supplies for his service brothers. The man who changed light bulbs. (Where did he take all the old bulbs?) The man who tossed his crutches aside and chose to sit on his knees all day and polish brass. The man who loved to drive a topless van of tourists around and challenge them to feel as passionate as he did. They each had a purpose. But more than that, they each *cared* about something. I thought about them all on that three-mile hike back to my son's apartment. I also thought about the plastic flowers in Hollywood Forever, as well as the plastic owl perched seven stories up—lifelike, but lifeless. Serving a purpose, but not capable of caring.

I stopped at the same market where I'd begun the day with a cold drink. My old friend was still there behind the counter. His face brightened when he saw me and he said, "I remember you!" Only in not as clear English as I'm able to write here. "You paid for drink for . . . for . . ."

"For that thirsty man," I said.

"Yes. The thirsty man." He said a lot of things after that, but because of his accent I could only make out bits and pieces. I learned he came from Sri Lanka, but I couldn't understand how long ago. "That thirsty man," he returned to what had happened earlier that morning. "He was not king. He was not poor." He seemed to think for a moment, maybe searching for the right English words. "He was human. I give drink and I give food," he placed a hand over his heart, "if I can help. But," now he held up a finger of warning, "not *all* the time!" Now he smiled and it was beautiful, even though his teeth were yellowed and some of them were broken. "I give without hoping back." He signaled back and forth with a wave of his hand. "I know God is watching on you."

I thought I had heard his admission about God. Thought I had sensed his connection to the God of heaven. But I wanted to be sure, so I asked, "*Who* is watching?"

"God," he repeated and pointed to the ceiling of his little shop, although it was obvious he was pointing way beyond the old wood overhead. "God is watching on you."

I immediately loved the once-confusing syntax of my new friend. "Yes, yes he is." And I shook his hand and introduced myself and asked him his name.

"I am Mr. Godfrey."

I'm willing to bet he didn't leave Sri Lanka with that name—a name that is now dear to me.

I said goodbye to Mr. Godfrey and stepped out of the market and turned up the street to where my son lived, past a historical building where I read F. Scott Fitzgerald once lived as he worked on *The Last Tycoon*, and a block away from where he died of a heart attack. A block away in a different direction was where my son lived. I would take him to dinner that night, I decided, and prompt him to get a haircut.

Because those are the sort of simple things people do who care about the living.

—

I fear not dying, but of never having lived.

—Marcus Aurelius

—

18

Zombies Don't Hike

Back when I was alive, I set out on a journey with my friends Dale and Larry up to the eastern most part of Tennessee to hike a section of the Appalachian Trail, only about twenty miles of the 2,180 mile total. It was summertime, so we wore shorts and sleeveless shirts. Larry's wife dropped us off on the side of the road at a spot Larry okayed. "This'll work," he said. He opened his backpack and began to hand Dale and myself some of the food he'd packed—cans of beans, some pasta sauce, a package of steaks, red and juicy-looking beneath the cellophane. "If we're going to be here for just three days, I want to eat good," he said. We all agreed. Sounded smart. "All right," Larry said, hoisting his lightened load onto his back. "Let's head up." And he took off into the woods. Dale and I hoisted our now-heavier packs and followed.

Right away I could tell this wasn't right—the trail, that is. It was too steep! Most of the time I was crawling like a crab, grabbing hold of saplings and roots, and if I ever stopped to catch a breath—which was often—scotching myself against large rocks to keep from rolling back down and undoing all the hard work. I could see Larry up ahead, moving goat-like, switching this way and that, using the land and trees to pull himself along. I should do that, I thought—as I hung onto a moss-covered stone and gulped air. Up ahead Dale had his arms circled around an oak. His breathing, indicated by the rising and falling of the backpack that was very in-sync with my own, told me he was still alive.

Slowly we scrambled up this mountain's face until we came to the top, about 6,500 feet high. There was a clearing and a barn-like structure at the edge of it. "It's the highest shelter on the entire Appalachian Trail," Larry told us. All I knew was that it was the first time in the last hour and a half that I could stand up and not worry about falling off backwards. I told Larry that the AT was much tougher than I had imagined. "Oh, that wasn't the trail," he said. "Kind of a short-cut just to get to the trail. You hungry?" and then he opened his backpack and pulled out the package of red meat—a bubble of protein and blood that made my stomach growl.

Four other hikers were already there and had struck up a fire. We introduced ourselves and crowded in around the warmth. Not much sun was left and so we scrambled for some utensils to cook our steaks— long sticks we could spear the meat with and stand back so we didn't burn our knuckles. "Are those steaks?" one hiker named Alan asked us. "Yeah, T-bones," Larry said as he ran a hickory branch through the center of one. Alan was spooning in some soup he'd warmed up over a propane stove.

Dale, Larry, and I stood circled around the fire with our spears bowed with the weight of our dinner. The sky had turned dark and we used our flashlights to check the progress of the cooking. "It's not easy to cook a steak over an open fire," Larry said. I knew what he was talking about. My steak turned black on one side so I spun the spear and torched the other side. Looked good to me. I pulled it from the flames and took a bite. The black, crusty skin was satisfying and tasty. Below that was red and bloody and spongy. Hmmm. I ate the scorched part, making circles around the steak as if it were corn on the cob, then reintroduced the steak back into the fire. "It's not easy cooking a steak over an open fire," I said, now with an experienced voice. I ate the steak in layers, as did Dale and Larry. Alan spooned in his soup, eyeing us, coveting the steak, I was sure.

When I was finished, I tossed in my spear and watched it burn blue and orange. My stomach was full, my muscles tired, my chin and fingers greasy. That night we slept in the highest structure on the Appalachian Trail—and mice raided our backpacks. "Any food you have," Alan told us as he boiled an egg on his propane oven the next morning, "you need to hang on the lines above." I thought it was a clothes line, for drying hand-washed clothes. But since we weren't near a stream, I realized that didn't make sense. We found new spears and Larry showed us how to pack the biscuit dough around them and cook them over an open fire. Biscuits on a stick. Much like the steaks, I ate my biscuit in layers—crispy then gooey. Alan, sucking back a boiled egg, watched every move we made.

The famous Appalachian Trail, at least the section in the farthest most part of East Tennessee, is not much more than a foot path. Filled with biscuits and jelly, Larry, Dale, and I headed north. Through crowded woods and open expanses, over roots and under low branches we hiked. Around noon we walked out into what is called a bald spot—treeless. We shed our backpacks and used them as pillows as we laid there and soaked in the sun . . . and ate Vienna wieners.

"Doesn't get any better than this," I said, fishing out the last of the wieners from the tiny aluminum can, contemplating drinking the wiener juice.

"Nope," Larry said, drinking down the wiener juice.

"Anybody got a pen?" Dale said. He's a songwriter and suddenly, there in the sun, on the mountain, in the midst of the temptation of wiener juice, he was inspired.

A couple of hours later, and maybe three miles from the bald spot, we came upon a small shelter that housed a book for hikers to sign. So we stopped and signed our names to the long list of other hikers. I thumbed through the pages. Listed here were the names of hundreds of hikers who'd been in this very spot. Maybe they hadn't eaten steak or biscuits or wieners. Maybe they had only eaten jerky and boiled eggs. But we'd shared this trail, this part of it anyway. This one moment where we stopped and said, "Hey, I'm going to write my name on this line." This act made me feel like I belonged to something much larger than myself. I was documented. I was on this trail. I had stamped the same ground as all these other names. Then Dale had an idea.

"Hey, let's see how many pull-ups we can do," he said, as he kicked aside his backpack and hopped up to the low-hanging timber just above our heads. He did twelve pull-ups. Larry was next and did ten solid pull-ups. Now, at this point I had no other options but to kick aside my backpack and leap up to the timber. No way I could say, "We need to get back onto the trail, guys." So I shed my pack, hopped up enough to barely grasp this beam—that held my weight just fine—and pulled up. I think I did eight, maybe six, but at least five good ones.

"Let's get on down the trail, guys!" I had the right to say now, and we hoisted our packs and moved on.

We hiked about twelve miles that first day and did about twenty-six pull-ups—collectively. Our second night there we would spend in an old barn dressed up for trail hikers. It was big and red and set in the middle of a vast, grassy area, close to a cold stream. When we reached this spot, late in the day, other hikers were already there. Alan was one of them. A fire was already blazing, so we cozied up and grabbed some warmth.

Larry procured the large pot from Dale's backpack and loaded it with noodles and water and parked it in the open fire. Tonight was pasta night. "Is that spaghetti?" Alan asked.

"Yep," is all Larry said.

After we were all carbed up, there was still enough daylight left to pull off a great sweat lodge. That had been Larry's idea all along. That's why he'd stuffed a big green tarp into his backpack and schlepped it this far. Larry dropped some big rocks into the fire and made sure they stayed near the hottest center. We found an old piece of metal and pulled it up to the barn. Then Larry fished the hot rocks out with a couple of big sticks and put them on the metal. When he unfolded the tarp he asked Alan if he'd like to join us. Alan, always a bit stand-offish, said, "No thanks. You guys giggle a lot."

So the three of us, Larry, Dale, and myself, covered ourselves with the tarp. It was dark and stale under there. Until Larry poured a few ounces of water onto the hot rocks. It was still dark, but now steam boiled out and surrounded us with its blistering heat. Dale giggled. I might have too. Larry kept pouring. The heat seared us, wrapped us up, and made it hard to breathe. Larry kept pouring. Dale giggled again. I might have too.

We sucked in the steam that boiled off the rocks. Our pores certainly opened up, and, to understand the science of what happened there, I would have to surf Google later. All I know is that it was hot and stifling. Larry kept pouring. We wore only our shorts. It was hot and wet. I could have been a dish in a dishwasher. Larry just kept pouring water.

When we peeled the tarp back, cold mountain air chilled us. We dried ourselves with dirty clothes and pulled on clean sweatshirts. Alan stood off and watched us. He seemed consternated. That is, until Larry hiked down to the stream and brought back the big pot he'd carried down earlier, before the sweat lodge moment. He dolloped out big spoonfuls of a sweet substance onto our somewhat clean dishes.

"Is that cheesecake?" Alan asked.

"No-bake cheesecake," Larry told him. "Want some?"

With that offer, Alan moved closer and extended his dish.

Yeah, I was alive then. Very much so.

As a zombie, I read a story about a man who had died the year before.

A local coroner said he starved to death—this man I read about in the newspaper, as I sat in a hotel lobby in the shadow of Pikes Peak in Colorado Springs. His name was Winston Branko Churchill and the news story said they'd found his body only three weeks before, about two hundred miles from where I sat. But he'd started his journey only about twenty miles from this same hotel lobby. He entered the woods one day—alone—and walked alone, ate alone, slept alone, then stopped eating—still alone. The woods stripped away his warmth, offered him a chilled ground to lie upon, and then covered him with about twenty feet of snow for the duration of the winter. Some hikers found him months later. He was still alone.

Ten years before this trip to Colorado Springs, my daughter Chera had a wild idea. She was fifteen when she came into my office one day and said, "Dad, I want to climb a mountain." She was determined and prepared. "There's a mountain in Colorado called Pikes Peak," she informed me. "There's even a walking trail all the way to the top. With a souvenir shop that serves ice cream." I wondered, *How hard could that be?*

So we bought matching backpacks, ordered a couple of plane tickets, and flew to Colorado Springs. We hailed a cab to take us to the trailhead. There's a sign at the beginning of the trail that says if you maintain a "brisk pace," you can reach the summit in eight hours. It took us *three* days! In those three days we learned about the sudden shift in altitude and what that can do to your sinuses. We got bruised up and sprained and exhausted beyond belief. But we did it. We had such an incredible experience that I came home and wrote about it and it became the first chapter of a book published by WaterBrook Press called *Don't Let Me Go.* It chronicled the next three years of climbing four more mountains and running in two marathons and watching my little girl grow into a beautiful young woman.

That was ten years ago when Chera and I set out on our own. Since that time thousands of people have read the book, and my little girl grew up and married. We wanted to do something special for that ten-year anniversary, so we planned a return trip to Pikes Peak. Only this time we brought her new husband Craig, and my son Zachary, who was nineteen now—too young to have gone with us the first time. As word got out about our climb some called and asked if they could come along. Absolutely, we said. The more the merrier. When we made our way to the trailhead early that August morning, there were thirteen of us. And it was indeed merry.

Churchill used to be a disc-jockey in Denver and then he owned a coffee shop in Silverton. Then he wanted nothing to do with materialism. His sister told the newspaper that he wanted people to change, to not get "caught up" in fancy homes and cars and money. But because he couldn't convince people of this, she said, he wound up "checking out."

We checked out of the motel early that morning—ten of us. Chad Molitor and his wife Shelly are in their early forties. They read the book, even all the parts about the battering, jarring, pain, and the grueling struggles and said, "We'd like to go with you back to that mountain." They brought Bree, their eighteen-year-old daughter. Ashley Giamo is Chera's friend, who used to be her boss at the bank where she worked. She'd read the book too and said "count us in." She and her husband Joey are in their mid twenties. Katie Keagen came along too. She's an old friend of Chera's, about Zach's age. And some from WaterBrook Press (located in Colorado Springs, in the shadow of Pikes Peak) met us there:

Steve Heron and Joel Ruse and his wife Breanne. So the thirteen of us met up at the trailhead, and wrestled with our packs, filled our water bottles, posed for pictures, and kept bumping into one another because it was rather crowded there at the beginning of the trail.

Our packs were the heaviest as we trudged up those first seven miles to a place called Barr Camp, where we had reserved a bunkhouse big enough for ten people. And since there were thirteen of us, some of us slept on the floor. So at bedtime, we were wall to wall in there.

At Barr Camp we took turns filling our water bottles from the stream that raced by the cabin, and dropped in iodine tablets to kill the bacteria. The camp managers made us spaghetti (the same recipe Chera and I had experienced ten years before!) and we ate until we couldn't move. Someone plucked a guitar from where it hung from a nail on the wall and passed it to Chera and she played stuff we all knew and could sing to. We were tired and sleepy and it wasn't even eight o'clock yet. But it was dark and that was good enough.

Even though we were at 10,000 feet, the bunkhouse was warm enough that we had to open the door. I peeled a corner of my sleeping bag back just enough so that I could feel an occasional passing of a cool breeze.

It still wasn't late, but we were exhausted and the next morning we had plans to head out early to reach the summit by the afternoon— about a five-hour hike.

"Let's play twenty questions," Katie said into the darkness.

"Okay," Bree answered. "I'm thinking of a person."

"Is it a woman?" Shelly asked.

"Yes."

"Is she dead?"

"Yes."

"Famous?"

"Yes."

"Amelia Earhart?"

"That's incredible!" Bree exclaimed.

"Come on!" A collective protest went up. "There's no way you can guess that in three questions!" If it weren't completely dark, I'd have suspected some sort of secret hand signals.

I wondered if Winston was ever warm enough. I imagined the night air, night after night, wrapped around him—patiently waiting for an opportunity to slip through the smallest of openings and steal pockets of his heat. Did he look up at the constellations? Could he call them out by names? There's Orion! Cassiopeia! Hercules! But then again, even if he could have called them out, or did call them out, there was no one there to hear.

At some point we switched games. We took turns thinking of movie titles and giving out just the initials. I wasn't exactly the best at this. When it was my turn I started—and rather slowly, because I had to think of the first letter of each word—"G . . . W . . . T—"

"Gone With the Wind!" Chad called out.

And that's how we fell off to sleep that first night—voices commingling with a cool welcomed breeze that passed through the entrance. The last thing I remembered was Steve, bunked just above me, saying something about cartoons.

Near the top of Pikes Peak the trail cuts back and forth in a most deliberate zigzag on the right face of the mountain. Then the trail suddenly turns left and makes a long, bowed scar across what would be its forehead, for at least a half-mile. Chera, Craig, Zach, and I had just made the turn when I heard someone call Zach's name. Way on the other side of the mountain I saw a figure skylined on a ridge—what looked to be, from where I was, the very edge of the mountain. I guessed it was Bree. That's what everyone else said too. Looked like her and sounded like her.

"Zach!" she called again, and this time she waved her arms and her voice flew over the surface of the mountain, paying no attention to the myriad switchbacks. We waved back. We called back. Zach would never say it, but there had to be something comforting in the idea that the surrounding rocks knew his name. That the sound of his name had been spoken (*shouted!*) by someone who shared this journey with us.

We made it to the summit, all but crawling those last few switchbacks. And there we shared cheeseburgers and fries and ice cream and doughnuts and chocolate with each other, and hundreds of others, who visited the souvenir shop—arriving via train or by car. We stayed about an hour and then it was time to go, only now we were stuffed full with food and accomplishment. The hike back to camp is when we were besieged by blisters. I carried the first aid kit, so I made many stops and watched as Chera patched up many toes and heels. We stayed there in our over-sized cabin again that night, and again fell asleep to the sounds of more guessing games.

They found Winston Branko Churchill on the ground near a locked cabin. The local coroner said he died of starvation and exposure. Inside the cabin was food. Some say he went off to die, that he wanted to. Others say he changed his mind at the last moment because they found the tip of his ski pole bent. Speculation was that he'd been trying to pry open the cabin door.

Someone saw Winston a few days before he died—an outfitter who manages some of the land where Winston was hiking. The witness said the man he saw (who was most likely Winston) seemed incoherent, tired, and wet. He offered him food and a place to stay. He even offered to look at his map and at least let Winston know where he was. But Winston had walked on. "I don't know what else I could have done," the witness said, "except grab him."

Grabbing him does sound a bit extreme.

The next day, somewhere back below the tree line, I found myself at the end of our line of thirteen. Chera was leading the way. The trail was such that I could see everyone, the backs of their heads at least, their jostling backpacks, and the unevenness of their downhill gaits. Ten years before Chera and I had made this same trip. Now we were separated by eleven people, and of those, only one did we know then—my son Zach. The rest we'd met over the last few years or months. One of them Chera had married. I inhaled deeply and was glad no one could see my face at that moment. *Dad, are you crying?* I could imagine Zach saying, with just an undercurrent of ridicule in his voice. *No I would say. This is what happiness looks like! This is what being alive looks like!* Then I would give him a big hug right there in front of everyone, embarrassment or not. But then the trail bent to the right and slowly, one by one, my friends began to disappear.

With great effort, I resisted the urge to reach out and grab anyone.

Our trip up and back down Pikes Peak was all about a crowded bunkhouse and spaghetti dinners at 10,000 feet; about Zach stopping from time-to-time to swing his backpack around and ask me to grab his water bottle for him; about Craig, a mile from the summit, looking upward and exclaiming, "This is the hardest thing I've ever done in my life"; about Chera cutting curious shapes out of the moleskin we used to patch up blisters; about Joey and Ashley slipping on Nashville Predators hockey jerseys at the summit for a photo op (and maybe free hockey tickets!) and applauding them for being so clever; about Joel half-carrying his wife Breanne down the mountain because her blistered feet were too tender to walk on; and Shelly and her daughter Bree giving her their extra socks so she could walk sock-footed the rest of the way down; about Katie sharing her Ben-Gay, and most of us taking her up on it; about Chad giving a stranger twenty bucks to carry his backpack down those last three miles because his knees had blown out (he didn't ask us because he believed we'd make fun of him—no way, buddy. I won't say a word!); about seeing a beautiful reunion with Steve and his wife and their three beautiful girls (who we'd heard so much about on the mountain); about thirteen of us being together for the long weekend and sharing. The mountain was just background.

For several months now, I've carried with me that newspaper that tells the story of how Winston Branko Churchill starved to death. I've read the article over and over. It's yellowed and the edges are rolled and frayed. The story is fascinating and disturbing at the same time. Fascinating in that a man desired more than anything to connect with people, and disturbing because it proved impossible for him. That he starved for food is true, and that's the science of it. But he also starved for companionship, and that's the heart of it. I imagined him standing there, maybe only a mile from the end, and saying into the emptiness, "This is the hardest thing I've ever done in my life." Only there was no one there to hear him.

I will toss away this old newspaper now because the yellowness of it saddens me. And I will call Chad and maybe we'll go have lunch and talk about our time on the mountain. And laugh about who snored the loudest. And fight over the check. And I also want to make sure it's okay to write about how he paid some stranger $20 to carry his backpack down the mountain. I wouldn't want to lose a good friend over something like that.

Today I am feeling quite full—and alive.

⁓

[Abraham] concluding that God is able to
raise up [Isaac] even from the dead.

—**Hebrews 11:19** WEB

⁓

Death of
the Zombie

I awoke one recent morning and decided to travel to the country—to the place where my father is buried. He'd died nearly thirty years before, when he was fifty-three. I'm fifty now, and so when I look into a mirror, I can see his face. And I'm often reminded of how, more than once as he wrestled with his demons, he told me, "One day you'll understand." I wasn't exactly sure what he was talking about then, but thirty years later, after times of celebration and moments of heartache and sometimes long periods of just hanging on by my fingernails, I was beginning to "understand": he was speaking about life and how tough it can sometimes be. And I think in his own way, from a place of hurt and pain, he was trying to tell me to hang in there, that I can make it. So I just wanted to thank him.

I live just outside of Nashville and my father is buried in Pulaski, Tennessee, near the Alabama state line, only about sixty-five miles from my house. I hadn't been to the site in about ten years—when I took my children who had never met him. That day, standing next to his grave with Chera and Zachary, who were easily distracted by the grave stones—the names carved in them, the crooked rows of gravesites, the wind, a butterfly—I tried to say something profound. But I think it came out more like reportage: *and then we carried the casket up here and the ground was all soggy and umbrellas were up. . . .*

So on a clear, crisp day in October I set out for my father's grave, about sixty-five miles away. One hundred and twenty miles later I was at a Kangaroo Market asking a stranger for directions to the Mt. Zion Baptist Church. (At least I had remembered the name.) For the last hour I had turned down many wrong roads. Some sights looked vaguely familiar, others not at all. I made u-turns, I turned around in strangers' driveways, I pulled to the side of the road and chastised my GPS for not knowing where Mt. Zion Baptist Church was. I was lost and searching for a gravesite.

The face of this stranger I had asked directions of lit up with recognition. "Yes," she said, "I know where that is. They built a great big new church there. Right next to the old one." I did not know about this.

"Maybe," I said. "But I'm looking for that old church, with a cemetery surrounding it. Lots of old graves." My father's being one of them, but I did not say this. I remembered, as a child, seeing some weathered, canted headstones that told me some of these dead had been born in the early 1800s and died before 1910. That always amazed me—all the life that had taken place long before I was ever thought of.

"Yes," she answered. "The old church and graveyard are right next to the big, new church."

So I took her directions: "Follow 31A and go through the square. Keep right. When you come to the triangle [here she made a triangle with her hands to aid me], still keep to the right. You can't miss it." The "you can't miss it" part was the only part that worried me. When someone says something like that, you usually always miss it.

So I drove through the square of Pulaski, Tennessee, remembering how, when I was a kid, my mom and dad would walk us around this courthouse, stopping in many of the shops. I remembered, for the first time in forty years, buying marbles—all glassy and slick—and trying to figure out the game of marbles that my Dad had described to me. But no one I knew played marbles, so I could not duplicate his early happiness. Dad and I would always step down into the basement of this old courthouse to pee at urinals that were twice as tall as myself.

I remembered the Sam Davis Hotel that we visited when my Dad owned a salvage store in Nashville. They were tearing the hotel down at the time and doing away with everything inside. We'd come with a big truck and loaded all the TVs from the hotel into the truck bed—stacked them up like bales of hay and tied them down with ropes. Someone with that many TVs should have been rich! I was ten?

Away from the square, nearly to the interstate, one road looked greatly familiar. It led me off the main road, up a steep incline. *This* was the road we'd taken on the day of his funeral. Things from that day were blurry, but not this steep road. Only it was graveled then. Now the narrow strip of asphalt led me through the trees, around a bend, and past a giant brick building that looked like a church—because of the steeple, glass, and an A-shaped entryway. The sign out front let me know it was indeed the Mt. Zion Baptist Church. But I didn't see what I'd come for. I slowed. I looked. Then I drove on. Must be somewhere else, I thought. So I returned to the main highway. Five miles later I was at the interstate, about to turn up the ramp, when I made a greatly illegal u-turn, sliding through the gravel on the shoulder of the highway. "She said the old church was next to the new church!" I said to the windshield.

"It has to be there. Maybe I didn't look good enough." I sped up on the way back, anxious now because I'd been driving for almost three hours.

When I approached the church this time, it was from a different angle—one that showed me the area behind the church, where the old church and cemetery sat as it had for over a hundred years. I wept as I pounded the steering wheel, surprised by the emotion, glad my children weren't there just then. I parked the car in front of the old church and recalled how that day, as my father lay in the tiny building with choir singers harmonizing from the other side of a curtain, hidden to us, the storm that raged outside had killed the power, and I'd tried hard not to read too much into the moment.

Then I recalled how we walked from the front door of the church to a site just across the way, near where his mother and father had been buried, where every May, as a child, we would come and visit and place flowers and then have a picnic—over there—in the clearing next to the older graves.

I headed out, but things had changed. There used to be a fence row here, I thought, next to this line of big oak trees. On the other side had been field and weeds. Now the fence row was gone and the weeds mowed and the cleared land was spotted with newer-looking graves. I was sure Dad's site was near this old fence row. But I couldn't find it. I walked to the end of the cemetery. Too far. I knew he wasn't this far down. Where? Slowly I walked the tree line. Reading the names as I passed: Bennett. McNeese. Beard. Britton. And finally . . . Pierce. My grandmother. And my grandfather.

Next to the granite marker was a flat bronze plate covered with leaves and a large stick. When he died I'd promised myself I would buy a big headstone. I still believe I will someday. I swept the leaves and stick away with my hands to read my father's name. And I wept some more. I felt foolish and hoped no one was watching. I plucked back the

Bermuda grass, thankful that the groundskeeper had not let it knit over the plate, as it easily could have, then took a few more pictures and told Dad that things were going well. "I've had some hard times," I told him. "But you knew that I would, didn't you? But that's just a part of being alive, right? I think I understand that now." That was as profound as I could get. Then I crossed my arms and covered my mouth so that it would appear to anyone watching that I was merely deep in thought.

I left after a few minutes and promised myself again that I would look into a new headstone. That would be nice. And that's probably easier to do now with all the online shopping opportunities we have.

On the way home I made a phone call to my daughter. She had not known where I'd been, or of the detritus I'd swept away from a grave marker earlier. She had company that day—friends full of life and energy who would break bread with her and her husband later. We would not climb a mountain that day, but I would remember the steep climbs, the sore muscles, and the smiles we had exchanged in thin air. Her life continues to bless me. I could end this story here.

Then I called my son, but his whispering words told me he was in class. "I'll call you later," he told me. My hands smelled of dying leaves. We would not ride a roller coaster that day or play Guitar Heroes. But I could remember the thrill of falling hundreds of feet, locked arm-in-arm with him, my eyes watering so much that only two feet away, he was just a blur. And I could remember my fingers tangling up trying to find the correct notes of a Lynyard Skynyard song, and Zach just laughing. I could end this story here, thinking of Zach.

Then I called my wife and told her what I had done. She said I should have taken someone. I shouldn't have done that alone. But I believed I had taken someone. I'd had a car full of people with me on that long trip! A good friend who may lose his car in parking garages—but still finds time to phone me to say hello; a gang member who gave me a welcoming fist pump to Los Angeles; buddies I'd shared air with as we swam to the ocean floor; Bob, the teacher who thought he might die that day and so had entrusted me with his lesson plan; a homeless man named Larry; the ghost of a man who had once changed light bulbs on the famous Hollywood sign; a store clerk from Sri Lanka named Mr. Godfrey, who always tried to help thirsty people; friends I'd scaled mountains with, and shared blisters with. They were all there that day, huddled around me as I brushed back that single stick and wept.

So I drove home, feeling victorious at having found my father's grave, at knowing my children were living life, grasping at all they could. And as I drove, I thanked God for his people—*all of them.*

Only two days later, I rapped on a door and it swung open and there stood my daughter, holding another human being in her arms. He was only about eight pounds, so it wasn't that difficult for her to do. Years ago I'd held her the same way. Over the years her soul has filled up with life. She shares it, takes it, loves it, and lives it. And now she has given it. His name is David Sawyer and we call him Sawyer.

Here is where this story should end, I believe.

I was once alive. Then somewhere along the way I died. I lost touch with those around me, those that mean the most. But what I discovered is that just as you can lose touch, you can gain it back. All you have to do is reach out, like Sawyer does.

I held him that day and could feel, against my chest, the heat of life emanating from his tiny body. His eyes were open and searching. There's no way he could have known what he was looking at—only lights, shapes, images, vague colors. And his arms were flailing about, little hands clasping and unclasping. "Just grabbing at air," some might say—a stranger who doesn't know him, who doesn't know me. But what

I saw then was a new human being, who is only doing what every human should do—old or new: grab up all the life you can. Reach out and grab it with all the enthusiasm of a twelve-day old baby.

That's what it takes to kill a zombie.

Afterword

I want to know Christ and the power
of his resurrection and the fellowship of sharing in his
sufferings, becoming like him in his death,
and so, somehow, to attain to the resurrection
from the dead. *[emphasis mine]*

—Paul, Philippians 3:10-11

I repeat this scripture, not because I have forgotten it, but because it bears repeating. I have felt dead for a long time—totally unengaged, and helpless about how I could come back to life, or if that was even an option. We love God through his people; God loves us through his people.

Because of this new-found knowledge, I now revel at the opportunity of being in the company of others. When the wife says, "Would you like to get together with _____?" my answer is always, "Yes."

When we are with others, we are alive. Only in this setting do we have the opportunity to be *resurrected*.